I0467826

Franchisees

What You Need to Know About Franchising

By

CSTI Business Training

All Rights Reserved 2014

Contents

"It is better to know things up front in life instead of learning them after the fact."

Disclaimer

The writers of this book are not accountants or lawyers and their suggestions and ideas should be used as the sole basis for any kind of commitment or business decision. Those types of decisions should be made by qualified people with the knowledge and expertise required to properly and effectively guide individuals based on their own specific set of circumstances. The information contained in this publication is designed to provide insight and awareness. Neither the writers, publishers or distributors of this book assume any responsibility for athe use of any or all parts of this book.

Introduction

Franchises have been around for a very long time. They are found in almost every industry and in almost every part of the world today. Some have instant name recognition while others might be local or regional businesses. But no matter their size or geography, all franchises share some common factors and business structures.

It is the purpose of this book to look at the franchise model closely and fairly. We are not out to attack the franchise model or to champion its strengths. Instead we want to provide objective e information designed to help determine whether franchising is right for you or not. We are not going to make the decision for you but we will give you a ton of information on which to base your decision.

The fact is, franchising is not for everyone. Contrary to the articles and sales pitches you might see or read, owning a franchise is not like getting a license to print money.

The success of your franchise is going to depend on several factors many of which will be under your control and many that are not. First and foremost it is a business and subject to the same influences and factors that every business is subjected to.

Franchises do fail when certain conditions exist. We have all seen franchise locations go out of business just like other businesses. Just because you have the luxury of an established name does not insure your initial or continued success. It is important that you understand this before committing yourself and your money to any franchise.

But on the flip side, there are many people who have made a ton of money owning franchises. Many people start with one location and buy more and more as their financial situation improves. There are many of these success stories and most of those success stories are people just like you and I who had a dream and followed it. So even though there are risks involved in owning any business, there are rewards in it as well.

Throughout this book we are going to discuss several topics that pertain to owning a franchise. Many of these topics pertain to any type of business but we are going to discuss them from a franchise viewpoint. Do not think that any of these topics are not important or do not pertain to you. I assure you that EVERY topic or chapter in this book WILL pertain to you either now or in the near future.

The key to success in any business venture is knowledge and awareness. If you equip yourself going into your new business with the knowledge you need to make the right decisions in the beginning, you not only will increase your chances of success but also reduce the number of mistakes you make as well.

Shortening the learning curve and reducing mistakes saves you time, money and other resources. Often these differences can mean the difference between your ultimate success and failure. So take the extra hour to read through this book I its entirety. The information you get from reading everything will help you immeasurably later on as well.

If I had to give you just one important piece of advice right now it would be to keep your eyes and ears open and learn as much as you possibly can. Knowledge is never a waste even if you don't think something is important or relevant to you right now. The fact is, the more knowledge we get and the more diverse that knowledge might be, the better able we will find ourselves to make the right decisions is the least amount of time.

So now it's time to get started. But before we do, here are a couple of suggestions on how you can get the most out of this book.

It is written to help you get the best results in the shortest period of time but there are two things you can do to make your chances of success even greater.

First, it's perfectly fine to skip around and go to the chapters that you think might help you the most right now. Depending on your particular situation you might need specific information right now in order to help you make the right decisions.

We have designed this book so that the reader can read the chapters in any order they desire and still understand the content in that chapter. So you don't have to start at page one and read through to the end in order to understand the content.

Because of this, you might find a few things repeated throughout this book. That is not a mistake but rather done on purpose so that no matter where you start you will be able to understand what you are reading. It also helps us learn because repetition is one of the most effective methods of learning. So repeating important information helps you learn more and retain it longer.

So start wherever you want but make sure to read everything in the book. The book is not so long that reading everything will take you a ton of time. But reading everything will help you make better and more accurate decisions because you will have more knowledge at your fingertips.

The second thing you should do is after you finish reading the book go back to page one and read it again. This time, take notes and make the material you read relevant to you and your own situation. Take the concepts and information we discuss and think about how it applies to your particular industry, business and life.

This is important because when we make something relevant to us our brains pay more attention and retain the information longer and with greater accuracy. We remain motivated and are far more likely to be successful. As you will learn throughout this book, perception and effort are critical to anyone's success. So read it through again and this time, make it as real as you can for you and your life.

All right, we have laid all the groundwork and are finally ready to get started. Make note of the date and time right now because this is when your life might very well take an important turn towards success!

Part One:

Kick Starting the
Process

There Are No Guarantees

If you are one of those people who think that if you pay fees and join an existing franchise that you are guaranteed huge profits and a successful business, it is time to set the record straight so that you can enter into this whole process with wide open eyes and the correct perspective.

Successful franchises will do everything they can to provide you with products and services and a business model that has proven to be successful where it has been tried. But since this is YOUR business and it is located in YOUR location using YOUR employees, there are a lot of variable that can either help or hinder the business becoming successful.

For those who can follow directions to the letter a franchise can take a lot of the guesswork out of the process. But any reputable franchise will tell you that there are no guarantees

The only thing the franchise can do is provide you the association with their brand name and access to their products and business model or system.

After that it is up to you. Franchises that are successful in some areas might fail in others. Virtually all franchises will have owners and locations that fail. That is because there is a lot of human error and other variable involved. You cannot possible remove all risk and create something foolproof that will work perfectly every time. Prospective franchise owners need to understand this and have reasonable expectations.

As far as risk is concerned, if you align yourself with a good and stable franchise with a strong brand name you will have a much easier time getting your business started. But even a strong brand will not make up for poor service or human mismanagement.

In other words, if you are looking for a guarantee, opening a new business is probably not for you.

Franchise Advantages

For those thinking about going into business for themselves, franchises just might be the right answer. Here are some of the main benefits of joining a franchise rather than opening your own business and trying to go it alone:

Instant Brand Name Recognition

Franchise owners will have the benefit of having a brand name already known by most people. This will lead to a kind of built-in comfort level in your products and services almost from day one. Since most people will go with a known brand first, this can be a great help in starting your new business.

Proven Business Model

Most independent business gets started and go through a lot of trial and error.

Many things that seem like they should work turn out to be wrong and time and resources are lost. With a franchise, most of the "bugs" and mistakes have been eliminated and you are presented with a business plan and model that has been proven for a period of time to be reliable and successful.

Training & Support

As a new business owner, there will be a lot of things that you don't know about starting and running your business. Even if you think you know everything, trust me, you don't. When you purchase a franchise, you can rely on the experience and knowledge of those at the corporate level to not only help get you started but teach you what you need to know to move forward.

On-going support is usually part of the franchise package as well. This gives you someone to ask questions when things don't go as planned or as hoped. Having someone to run ideas past will save you and your business time and money and allow you to accomplish more in less time with better results.

Ready Made Product Line

One of the "headaches" when you have your own business is finding products and services that are proven sellers.

Even after you find your initial product offerings, you will need to create and introduce new products to keep your business fresh and current. When you are part of a franchise, product creation and development is taken care of for you.

In addition, finding sources for your products at competitive prices can be difficult as well. Plus, as an independent business, your purchasing power is limited and the vendor is not likely to care very much about you and your business. When you are part of a franchise, huge purchasing power allows the business to control the source and not vice versa.

Corporate or Group Advertising

The cost of developing and purchasing advertising can get to be very expensive. Franchises usually have pre made advertising materials and the ability to purchase large amounts of advertising on a national or regional basis for much less than individual businesses could. This will give you more "bang" for your advertising dollar.

Access to Expertise

With so much to handle and address during the starting of any business, it is nice to have people in your corner to advise you and answer questions

With a franchise, the parent company has a vested interest in seeing that you succeed. If you fail it is considered a black mark against the franchise and the brand itself.

That means the franchise is going to do their best to make sure everything is done right so that you have the best chance to succeed. They will have approved contractors and vendors as well as expertise on every aspect of starting the business to help you every step of the way. You don't get that when you are on your own.

Franchise

Disadvantages

While franchises offer some great advantages for many owners, they are not perfect and they are certainly not for everyone. You have to be a certain kind of person and business owner to thrive in the franchise environment. Whether or not you are that kind of person hopefully you will discover throughout reading this book.

All that being said, here are some of the disadvantages of owning a franchise:

Entrance Fee

In addition to all the costs of starting your own business, franchises charge a fee just for the right to use their name and logo and share in their business model. The fees will vary greatly and according to the size and brand name recognition. The larger and more successful the franchise, the more you will pay to join.

Fees ranging from $10,000 to several hundred thousand dollars or more may be charged just to gain entry into the franchise. This does not include buildings, products or licenses or anything else. This is just the fee to join the franchise. If the business should fail, or if you are unable to even get started, the fee may or may not be refundable.

On-Going Fees

In addition to the entrance fee most franchises also have monthly or quarterly fees based on sales or sometimes just flat rate fees. These are in addition to the entrance fees and are one of the ways the franchise itself makes money. These fees offset the costs of support and other activities that go on behind the scenes.

Loss of Total Control

While this is your business, you are using someone else's business model. You have to agree to follow that model as well as the rules and procedures outlined in that model. You do not have the ability or right to do anything you please when it comes to running a franchise business. You have to follow their plan and have anything outside that plan, or different from the plan approved before you can do anything.

Firm Business Model

If you don't like following orders or instructions, then franchising is not for you. Operating a franchise means doing what you are told when you are told and how you are told. Many people like this because it takes the guesswork out of what needs to be done. But other people absolutely hate following orders or instructions. If that sounds like you, think very carefully before making a commitment to any franchise!

Less Flexible

Part of the lure of owning your own business is not having someone telling you what to do like your old boss used to do. But with a franchise, you must stay within agreed upon parameters and will not have the open-ended flexibility you would have if this was your own independent business.

Sometimes this might become a problem if you see something that needs to be done differently in order to save your business but the franchise is unwilling to allow you to make the changes.

Security

Though no business offers any kind of guarantee when it comes to being profitable, franchise do give you better chances to success.

However, along with that success comes the risk of losing your franchise. Most agreements have clauses that allow the parent company to remove you from your franchise for various reasons. That means you could build a profitable business and then be stripped of it if you violate the terms of your contract.

This is great reason why your should have a good lawyer involved with your business to help advise you and protect you against the franchise coming after you for whatever reason.

Lack of Individualarity

When you join a franchise, you must agree to look like every other location and create the same environment that exists in all the other locations. You cannot do your own thing and grow your business your way. If that is something you like to do, then franchising might not be for you.

Termination

or Cancellation

Even though this is your business, registered in your name or company name, it is still part of a larger company and subject to their rules and regulations. When you sign your franchise agreement, you agree to follow their business model including all their rules, procedures and policies. If you fail to follow everything that you agreed to follow, you can be removed from your franchise.

This is not as threatening or as sinister as it first appears but it is something that you should be aware of from the very beginning. It just makes sense that individual franchise owners not be able to change things at their own discretion and damage the brand for everyone else. Because of this, there are usually termination or cancellation clauses built into every franchise agreement.

Your lawyer can make sure the language contained within the contract concerning termination or cancellation is specific and fair to both parties. They also should enquire as to what kind of process is followed when termination or cancellation becomes an issue. The last thing you want is an innocent mistake result in you losing your business because of unfair wording in the franchise agreement.

In addition, some franchise agreements run for a limited period of time. That is usually 10 or 20 years and then they come up for renewal. That means that you could develop a successful franchise business over the first 9 years only to have it not renewed or taken over by the company from that point forward. Though most franchises are not looking to displaced successful owners, it is best to have your lawyer look over the contract and advise you on how to best protect yourself.

We should also mention that not all franchises have limits on their agreements. Those that do primarily have them in there so they can eliminate problem owners who damage the brand or the businesses of other franchisees through unethical or suspect business practices. In those cases, the time limits help protect both the company and the other franchisees.

Surrounding Yourself with Success

Perhaps the best piece of advice I can give anyone thinking about going into any kind of business is to not be fooled into thinking that they know everything and can do everything themselves. Owning a successful business requires so many different skills and knowledge sets that it is almost impossible for any one person to do a great job at everything.

Plus, there is a little thing called time that often gets in the way as well. Even if you were the one in e million that was able to do everything better than anyone else, you still wouldn't have time to fit all that in on a daily basis.

So let's put the ego's to the side and admit that we are going to need help. We may not want help, but we definitely are going to need it.

The most successful people and companies today usually share one thing in common. They all surrounded themselves with people who had a higher level of skill at certain things than they did. They did not fool themselves into thinking that no one could do it better. Instead, the searched out the people with the best skill sets and hired them to handle parts of their businesses for them.

This allows more to get done in less time and with better or more accurate results. It allows businesses to change and adapt faster and enables the business to take advantage of trends and influences much faster than the competition. This makes the business more responsive to customer needs and the marketplace.

Do yourself a favor and decide what you are truly great at and stick to that as much as you can. If you are able, surround yourself with people who have the knowledge you need and learn from them. Be a sponge for knowledge and soak up everything people tell you. When it comes to business, the more you know the better off your business will be.

I also realize that sometimes businesses just getting started will not have the ability or resources to hire experts on everything. But expertise does not always have to come from employees or hired assistants.

There are local and state government agencies and business development programs that routinely offer assistance to small businesses.

Take advantage of any program or venue that gives you access to the skills and experience that might be lacking within you. Don't convince yourself that you know more than you do. In fact, convince yourself that you could use help everywhere. Improve every skill you have through reading books, taking courses and making yourself more knowledgeable and more valuable to your business.

The overall success of the business starts with the skills and abilities of its owner and how he or she deals with that. Do yourself a favor and surround yourself with people that will give you the best chance for success. You will be so glad you did!

Part Two:

Making Your Decision

What is a Franchise?

When you hear the term "Franchise" what images pop into your head? Most of us immediately go to the common fast food chains or restaurant chains. If that is what you thought of initially, you are right. Those are franchises. In its most simple definition, a franchise is a set of businesses in multiple locations that have the same name and business model but different owners in remote locations.

A franchise is really one large business model placed into action by different owners in different locations. That means people like you and I open a business using someone else's business name and business model.

The theory behind franchising is that someone without specific knowledge in how to establish and grow a new business can start their own business using someone else's expertise. They are, in fact, buying a business that someone else has created, refined, and made popular and profitable.

In short, franchisees are purchasing a business that has had most, if not all, the "bugs" worked out already.

That means that the person buying into the franchise gets what is hopefully a fully tested and refined business and marketing program. In fact, besides the use of the name, this tested and proven business model and plan are the most important parts of the process.

Naturally, all of that pre-testing and refinement of the business model is not free. When you buy a franchise you agree to pay a percentage of your sales or income to the franchisers every month or year or however your agreement indicates. There is also a substantial down payment or entrance fee as well. These fees and costs can be substantial and that is one of the drawbacks to purchasing a franchise instead of starting your own business outright.

The great thing about starting out as a franchise is that you already have an established name that will draw customers to your business. You will have customers who recognize the brand name and have faith in it. You will also know what to do with those customers as they walk through your doors. Despite the fees you will have to pay to the brand owners, this added traffic and customer base will usually more than defray the costs of the monthly fees.

As a franchise owner, you reap the rewards of growing a successful franchise. As your sales and business grows, so does your income. Instead of managing a franchise for someone else, you will reap the financial rewards of owning your business. However, you will also assume the liability if your business should falter or fail.

It is important to know and understand that all franchises are not the same and not all franchises have the same costs or fee structure. Generally speaking the largest and most popular franchises are going to cost the most money. So you have to make a decision of whether you want to pay higher fees from the start or get in on the ground floor of a new franchise where the fees are lower but the risk of failure might be higher.

The ideal or perfect franchise model is where both the owners of the brand and the individual franchisees all make money every month. The brand owners get to expand their brand at a much faster rate by using the resources of individual owners and the individual owners get an established and proven business model.

This is franchising at its most basic level. IN the pages that follow we will explore the different aspects of franchising and how you should approach them and deal with them. But for now, we hope you understand at a basic level exactly what a franchise is and how they operate.

Why a Franchise?

For many people, the first question they ask themselves when thinking about purchasing a franchise is "Why should I pay fees to someone else every year when I could start my own business and keep all the profits?" Well, that is a very good question and unfortunately there is a pretty good and convincing answer to that question.

The harsh reality of it is that the vast majority of new businesses fail within the first year or two. They fail for various reasons ranging from poor business skills, lack of financing, poor business model, lack of training, lack of understanding, lack of support and a host of other reasons. The fact is, getting a brand new and different business off the ground and turning it into a success is not an easy thing. It is certainly not a slam dunk like many people believe. While there most certainly is a lot of money to be made in owning your own business, there are risks involved as well.

There are many skills necessary to create, build and maintain a thriving business. Very few people have all of these skills or the resources to hire people who possess these skills. Because of that, some new business owners try to do the best they can with limited or non-existent skills in some areas. In these cases, the business suffers.

For example, you might be great at creating the business model and designing the business plan but be really poor at sales or customer service. You might be really good at sales but clueless about how to market your business. This does not mean that you are a bad person or a poor business man. It just means that you are human. If you think you are great at everything, trust me, you are not. Accept that for now and get over it.

Franchise owners, however, do not have to be great at everything because a lot of the design and preparation for starting the business has been done already for you. If the franchise itself has been successful, it means the business plan is tested and performs well. It also means that it has been constantly improved and adjusted over time as the economy and marketplace changes. This hopefully has been done by people with specific skills designed to produce high quality and successful results.

The other great part of being part of a franchise is that the learning curve is extremely short when compared to someone trying to building their own business by themselves. Even the best minds and the smartest people make mistakes. They might look at a product or marketing campaign and think it is the greatest thing ever made only to see it flop or fail miserably. This happens to everyone every now and then.

But these mistakes have been made already for you by others and by the time you are joining they have established plans and procedures that have been proven to be effective and have also been proven to product the right results.

This can be especially helpful in the beginning when revenue is low and resources are tight. New businesses usually undergo a period where expenses exceed revenue because the business is not widely known or because the why the business is structured is not perfect. In other words, there is a learning curve involved in the start of every new business.

But a franchise, when built and developed carefully, can take that learning curve and shorten it dramatically. The name alone can help drive customers through your doors before you are able to attract customers on your own. You would be surprised to know just how valuable a brand name can be when people try to decide which restaurant or store to visit.

Franchises also have the ability to provide the new businessman with a tested and proven product. If the franchise operation is a quality operation with many locations, then it stands to reason that the products and services they market are of good quality and are reasonably well received by the customers. | This makes it a safer investment than trying to launch a new product or service and not knowing what the public reaction is going to be.

Franchises also have the contacts needed for you to turn your business from a blueprint to a brick and mortar reality. They may have construction plans for the building to vendors for the signage, graphics and other materials. They will also be able to either supply you with materials and supplies or set you up with vendors who are designated suppliers to insure consistent quality across franchise locations.

In addition for making it much easier to get all of these suppliers and contractors, franchises usually also negotiate rates based on franchise level buying power which might mean you can get supplies and materials cheaper through the franchise than you would if you were an individual business owner.

Another positive is that being part of a franchise gives you a better relationship with these contractors and suppliers.

If you were an individual business owner, your business might not mean much to the contractor and they might place your orders in the rear of the pile and take care of their larger customers. If you leave and go somewhere else, it would make little difference to them. But they will want to keep a large franchise account so they will likely give you better and faster service.

The same can also be said for marketing and advertising resources. Franchises usually have pre-made advertising programs and materials that are made available to franchisees. This can save the new business owner a ton of time and money because they do not need to create their own marketing materials. Plus, these are usually already pre-tested for performance. Another marketing advantage is that the cost of marketing can be much less when done on a large franchise wide scale. Franchisees usually pay a fee for advertising and all these fees are rolled into one national or regional advertising budget. So you might pay what might be the cost for one commercial and instead get 25 commercials! That is a great advantage for all the franchisees!

But perhaps the biggest positive aspect of owning a franchise is the training and on-going assistance you will get in starting your business, maintaining it, and growing it once it becomes established.

Make no mistake about it; franchises want you to succeed. They want your business to become successful because it is in their best interests to have you succeed. As a franchise owner, you will generate revenue and fees based on that revenue that will be paid to the franchise administration. The more revenue you generate, the higher the fees you will pay are going to be!

While that might sound bad to you, it really is not. Higher fees mean you are making more money. So if the check you write to the franchise this month is double what it was last month, that is because you made a heck of a lot more money this month than the month before! So the more successful you become, the more money the franchise administrators get in fees.

The other reason franchises want, even need, you to succeed is so that they can continue to sell more franchises! If they sell 100 franchises and 75 of them go out of business in the first year that is going to make it very difficult for them to make their franchise sound attractive to other potential investors. But if they sell 100 franchises and 98 of them do very well, they will have no problem attracting more investors and will even be able to charge larger fees!

Good franchises will have training programs and support in place to help individual franchises owners. These programs will give you the skills you need to get started and the on-going support you will need as you learn the practical aspects of owning and operating a franchise. If the franchise you are looking to invest in has no formal training or support structure, I advise you to look for another franchise.

One important part of the franchise experience is being able to talk and communicate with other franchise owners to discuss what works and what doesn't seem to work in your businesses. Business problems and successes are rarely unique so what one franchise owner has problems with others usually will experience the same problems in their location. So being able to share experiences and successes helps everyone to become more successful in less time.

Can You Develop or Find Quality Products that Sell?

OK, the heart and soul or every business are the products and services they offer their customers. If the products are good and of high quality and the prices are right, you might be on to something. But only if those products are right for the people in your area. Like we said before, if you are selling hang gliding equipment in a senior citizens area, good luck with that!

You have to have the products your customer need and want and they must be high quality and priced competitively. If you nail those three things, and not just two out of three, you have the makings of a successful business. The problem is that many people do not have the skills or know-how to develop the right products.

Franchises provide you with a set line of products that you can instantly sell to your customers. These products have brand recognition and have been proven to be successful elsewhere. So that is a big advantage to the new business owner. Plus, the franchise provides the materials and products to their franchisees so you won't have to worry about supplies and production hassles either.

Make no mistake about it, it takes a lot of time and money to design, test and produce a new product. Then you have testing to see if the product will be in demand and further testing to develop the proper price point. All of this takes time, knowledge and resources.

If you have your own products that you have designed and produced, then perhaps franchising is not the way for you to go. But if your plan is to find products that are already good sellers and bring them to the people in your town and do not want the hassles of finding those products, then franchising might be a good choice for you.

Why NOT a Franchise?

Everything in life has two sides and franchising is no different. There are negatives involved in owning a franchise. In addition to the fees and initial purchase price there can be other mandated fees and costs involved in owning the franchise. Always get a full disclosure before signing any kind of contract.

While a franchise owner owns his or her location, they do not have the freedom that a stand-alone business owner usually has. Franchise owners usually cannot sell other products or deviate from the franchise business model without formal approval from the franchise administrators. That goes for not only the products but the materials used and the vendors chosen.

Franchise owners must also be very good and very willing to take directions and follow them to the letter. While this might not be a problem for most owners, some might find this very difficult and want to make changes or take shortcuts. Not only will this stand in the way of your success, it could even result in the termination of your franchise.

You also have to realize that if other franchise owners do something that damages the franchise brand, they will be damaging your business as well. Your overall success or failure is definitely tied to the performance of the overall brand name.

So if someone owns 10 franchise restaurants and operates them in an unsanitary manner and people get sick, the brand, and your business are likely to suffer because of their actions.

Though this is unlikely with reputable and established franchises, you could have your franchise license revoked if you do something wrong or if your actions and location are determined to be a negative influence on the rest of the franchisees. This is usually spelled out clearly in the licensing agreement so make sure you understand that fully to protect your investment and your business.

Summary

Franchises represent an opportunity for a person to get into their own business without having to go it alone. Franchising isn't for everyone but for some people it is the perfect way to own your own business while getting the on-going support you need to stay profitable.

But all franchises are different and the prospective owner should investigate several different franchises in their industry before deciding which one they should buy into. There might be a wide range of fees and costs involved as well as other costs that might make one franchise a better fit than the others.

As with everything else when it comes to business, the best decisions are the ones that are made after carefully investigating each franchise and making informed decisions. Do not rush into purchasing your franchise. Think about it and investigate it carefully before making any commitment.

Is a Franchise Worth It?

This is a question most all prospective franchise owners ask themselves before deciding on whether or not to get into the franchise model of business. After all, there is a considerable investment made in purchasing and opening a franchise location. There are a few things to consider when it comes to deciding whether or not franchising is worth it for you and your situation.

As we stated, the value of a franchise opportunity lies primary in three areas. The first is the product or service you will be selling, the brand awareness and reputation of the product, and the support training and follow-up training provided. You will find that the most well known and respected franchises will excel at all three of these segments. All of these areas, plus a few more should be spelled out in their business plan.

Also to be considered are the assistance they will provide you in building your location and getting it ready for opening. This is a very critical time where specialized skills and knowledge is required and most people do not possess that kind of knowledge. So there is a value in that as well.

As we said, being part of a well known franchise can mean almost instant brand awareness and recognition for your business. If you are going to open a hamburger restaurant more people would be likely to visit your restaurant if you had the brand name like McDonalds than they would if your restaurant was called "John's Burgers". In the early stages of any new business, sales are going to be slower until word of mouth makes your business well known. Franchising will help you reduce that sales curve and there is a value in that as well.

Value will also be present in having tested and proven products and services to sell right from day one. You will not have to carry a bunch of products and wait to see which sell and which ones don't. That should have all been done for you by the franchise management and testing team. This means not having to waste time and money stocking the wrong products or inferior products.

The largest factor in deciding whether a franchise is right for you is whether or not it makes economic sense for you. For some of us, the franchise joining fee alone may be cost prohibitive. If that is the case then the decision has been made for you. If you can't afford it you either have to look for another opportunity or wait until you can afford it.

If you already possess all the skills and knowledge necessary for starting your own business maybe you don't need all the support and resources that franchising brings to the table for you. If you know how to market a business and how to build and establish a new business, perhaps you can avoid the fees and additional costs and go it on your own.

But the product issue might be the biggest stumbling block. Customers are product and brand driven people. They will drive right by an independent burger place and stop at the McDonalds. They will drive right by the mom and pop hardware store and stop at one of the hardware chains or big box retailers. They do this not because the service or product selection is any better but because they know what they will find in the name brand stores and they have a higher comfort level of finding what they need once they go into the store.

Perhaps the best example of the name brand value is with hotel chains

If you want to get into the hotel business, you almost have to go the franchise route with an established chain of hotels. You will need their reservation system and their marketing system to bring you guests from all over the world. No one from Los Angeles is going to book a room at Herb's Hotel when there is w ell known chain in the same area. To make matters worse, no one is likely to even know Herb's Hotel even exists!

From the customer point of view, a well known franchise gives the impression of quality and security. With a franchise you can pretty much assume you will get the same burger in Minneapolis that you got in Daytona Beach as long as you went to the same brand named restaurant. If you had a family of kids in the car, they would want to go to the franchised location instead of the local restaurant. That is because we have had it drilled into our brains through advertising and marketing.

All things considered franchising will give you the highest chances of success as long as you pick a quality franchise system. The most popular franchises will have the highest costs and fees but also the largest and strongest brand awareness. Franchises leave much less to chance than independent businesses do. All of this has a certain value attached to it.

If you feel that a franchise addresses some of your weaknesses or shortcomings then factor that in as well. As we stated already, no one is a master of everything and you should not expect yourself to be one either. But very few of us have unlimited resources either. We need to make informed decisions and understand the costs involved both at the beginning and until the business becomes self sufficient.

That is why it is critical to find a good accountant and business consultant. Someone who can take a look at the opportunity and your finances and let you know if this all makes sense on a financial level. Desire and work ethics are important but having enough money to see your business through the beginning stages is critical.

Many a great business model has failed because the business owner did not have sufficient capital or financing to see their business through the early days as sales and revenue were building. You cannot tell yourself that if your business needs $500,000 to get started that all you need is $500,000. You actually need much more to help market and sustain your business as it grows before it becomes self sufficient. Your accountant will be able to give you the information you need to make an informed decision.

Remember that different franchises have different costs and fees. If you cannot afford these expenses you should not enter into any agreement. You cannot hope that sales will come extremely quickly and that you will be able to pay the fees out of your profits. Granted that will happen eventually but you need the finances to sustain your business until that happens.

Do not enter any business arrangement, franchised or other if you are undercapitalized. It is much better to wait until you have the necessary funds to start and grow your business. Some franchises will offer you financing as well and this can take some of the pressure off you when you are just getting started. But make sure you are aware of the costs of this financing. Know the interest rate and terms and compare that to other possible sources of funds. You might find a better deal elsewhere. For example, a home equity line of credit might give you better terms and interest rates.

Summary

As to whether or not a franchise is worth it for you personally, only you and your accountant can make that decision. Weigh the value of using someone's expertise against using your own knowledge and experience.

Be honest with yourself and do not give yourself more credit than you deserve when it comes to skills evaluation. In the case of risking your life's savings, it is better to be safe than sorry.

Whatever franchise you do decide you are interested in, do your best to develop a level of confidence and security before making that commitment. Talk with other franchise owners and get their opinions. Remember the franchise owners are people like you and I and can give you an unbiased opinion. If you do go this route make sure that YOU pick the locations to visit and do not allow the company to direct you to certain locations. If you allow that to happen you will only get to see the best location and speak to only the most positive owners. You want an accurate cross-section of both the good and the not so good.

It is well worth taking the time to drive to several locations. Even if they are few and far between and it takes you a week to make your visits. This is your future you are talking about as well as a considerable investment on your part. You want to get the best and most accurate information possible on which to base your decision.

Remember the company administering the franchises are salesmen at heart. They are going to do their best to convince you to go with their company rather than another in the same marketplace or industry.

Everything is a competition and they are all competing to get your money. So do not take what they tell you as the truth. Question everything, have your accountant look at the paperwork and contracts and then and only then make an informed decision.

You Be Honest with Yourself?

Starting your own business of any kind can be a daunting and expensive process. This is true regardless of whether you go the franchise route or not. There will be a lot of time and effort and money involved in getting your new business started and you need to be aware of this from the very beginning.

This is not designed to scare you off or to convince you to not start your own business. It is designed as sort of a reality check to make sure you go into the entire process with your eyes wide open. This is critical because you will have to make decisions and the more you are aware of things the better the quality of the decisions you will likely make.

Being able to be brutally honest with yourself during every phase of starting and operating your business is a critical part of your success or failure. While sometimes it might be difficult to admit that you are lacking in any particular skill, it is important that you have a thorough understanding of your skills, strengths and most important, your weaknesses.

Starting and building a business requires a very diverse set of skills. You have to be able to understand and take part in marketing your business, negotiating contracts and prices, understanding local laws and building requirements, understand present and future financial needs and issues as well as being able to forecast future business and market place trends.

Then there is hiring of employees, customer service skills, and all the other skills and abilities your particular set of customers needs and requires. This includes product specific information, industry or market segment knowledge and the ability to understand your customer's needs and provide products and services that continue to address those needs both now and in the future.

The thing about building a business is that you must have ALL those skills and abilities. Having some of them will just not cut it. You must be able to handle ALL the responsibilities of the business or hire people who can.

The first step is the process is to really understand what you are good at and what areas you think you are lacking in and then take action.

Doing a thorough analysis and evaluation of your individual skills can be an eye opening and not all that pleasant experience. Admitting to yourself that you are not particularly good at something can be difficult. But it has to be done so we understand what areas we need to address NOW rather than later.

Throughout the process you need to be brutally honest with yourself. Do not pull any punches and do not assume you can do something you're not sure you can do. At this stage, it is far better to be overly critical or negative than it is to give yourself more credit than you deserve. In other words, it is far better to discover later that you actually knew more than you thought than it is to find out you knew far less.

This is also time to leave your ego at the door. You should not tell yourself you can do things you can't just to make yourself feel better. You should also not tell yourself you are willing to do things that you know you are not willing to do either.

For example, starting a business takes a LOT of time especially at the very beginning. Some business owners work 12-16 hours a day 7 days a week in the beginning until the business settles in and starts to earn a profit.

Are you willing to do that? Are you willing to work that long and hard to make your business succeed? Answer honestly because if you are not willing to put in the time and effort then you will likely have to make other plans to address this shortcoming.

Throughout this book we will cover a lot of different aspects of owning your own franchise business. But even though a franchise will help provide you with some of the knowledge and expertise you will need to get started, you will still have to have the ability to learn these things and handle them yourself or find people who will handle them for you.

Business owners will all tell you that even if you have people doing things for you, it is still a good idea to understand what they are doing and why they are doing it. Employees can come and go and the same can be said for partners as well. In the event someone should leave, get sick, or worse, you will need to be equipped to step in and handle things moving forward until a replacement can be found.

Even if the employee or partner remains with you, this is your business and you should understand how everything works so that you can avoid being cheated or robbed by people who are doing things you are not aware of.

So let's just say that at this point you need to understand your strengths and weaknesses compared to the skills you will need to start and operate your business. Write down everything you think you will need to do in order to run a successful business. Do not leave anything out no matter how trivial or small it might be. Sometimes the little things can make all the difference.

Then, after each item give yourself an honest evaluation. If you have great knowledge or skills at something, then indicate that. If your skills are kind of OK, indicate that as well. If you are totally lacking in something indicate that as well.

When you are done you will have a snapshot of your overall skill level as it pertains to the skills required to run your own business. This will give you a starting point from which to form an action plan. For skills that are not strong or totally lacking, you have two options. You can either hire someone to do these tasks or acquire that knowledge yourself. Sometimes new owners hire someone to help them get started and then take over those tasks when they become comfortable doing them by themselves.

Do not fall into the trap of convincing yourself that you can do something in order to save the money you will have to spend outsourcing those tasks to someone else.

This is a common trap and is the cause of many a business failing from the start. In the time between starting your business and having it become established, EVERYTHING must be done right to minimize mistakes and to cause sales to grow as quickly as they can. Trying to save a few dollars now can result in your business failing to gain traction in the market.

This is not to say that you cannot do everything yourself. Many people are capable of doing everything but choose to concentrate only on what they do best and leave the rest to others who can do the job better than they can. Others try and do everything themselves because of financial reasons.

There is no one right approach or answer to what is right for you. Only you can know what the right approach is for your situation. The best way to make the right decision is to be honest with yourself and listen to what others tell you as well. Ask other people what they think and do not get offended when they tell you something you might not wish to hear. Listen to their advice and the reasons behind it.

Then ask yourself what you think and be as open and honest as you possibly can. Keep in mind that you don't have to share this evaluation with anyone else. It can be strictly for your eyes only.

So there is no need to be embarrassed by what your determinations might be. But if your evaluation is open, honest and accurate, then your chances of moving forward in a positive and successful manner will be greatly improved.

Can You Afford it?

One mistake that potential franchisees, as well as people considering opening their own independent business, is whether or not you can afford to make this kind of investment or commitment at this time. There is a lot more to think about other than the franchise fee you have to pay to get your franchise license.

Every business, whether it is a franchise or an independent, is going to go through a period where incoming sales are lower than the costs of running the business. That means whatever profits are generated will not be enough to pay the rent, salaries, inventory, taxes and fees and any other expenses that are required. Depending on the type of business and the location you decide upon, there might be construction or building costs as well.

That means that you, as an owner, might not be able to draw much of a salary, if any salary at all, from your business for a certain period of time. In addition, it is likely that you will have to put money into your business for a while until it becomes self sustaining. There is no way of knowing for sure how long a period of time this will take. Every business and every location and every situation are different.

That is why perhaps the single most important piece of advice I can give anyone thinking about starting their own business is to get an account / financial advisor on board BEFORE you commit to any kind of business or franchise. Do this as one of the first things you do before signing any contract or making any kind of commitment.

Your accountant will do several important things for you. They will analyze your current financial situation to make sure you either have enough money or will be able to access the financing you need in order to properly start and open your business. They will tell you before you get started whether or not this is the right time for you to make this commitment.

They will also advise you on how to structure your finances and what you are likely looking at in terms of a total commitment to your new business.

That means any franchising fees and all other costs associated with opening the business before a single sale is even made plus all forecasted expenses until the business is forecasted to become profitable.

Some people might feel that the franchise people will be able to advise you and give you all the information you need upfront to make the right decision. But keep in mind that the franchise people have their own interests in mind first and foremost. While they might tell you that you are not ready because you are so undercapitalized that you present a danger to their brand, they are not as likely to tell you the complete truth for fear of scaring you away.

On the other hand, your accountant or financial advisor will have your interests at heart. They will be able to ask the right questions and see through any vague or questionable answers. More important, they will know what questions to ask and how to dig through mountains of financial information to uncover the information relevant to you.

They will also be able to advise you on what particular business or franchise choice might be the best option for you. If you want t open a burger franchise, for example, they might look at the largest 3 franchises and let you know which ones have the best business model and offer the best overall value for you. Then you can make an informed decision as to which is the best one for you.

Once you make your decision you are going to have to have an accountant anyway so it is best to get them involved sooner than later. Finances are an involved part of business and most of us have only a cursory knowledge of the basics. It is not a question of whether or not you can afford to hire an accountant. The question should be can you afford NOT to hire one in the beginning.

I also advise you to choose your accountant from a person recommendation from someone you trust. Do NOT use an accountant or advisor chosen for you by the franchise owners! While they probably will recommend someone who is good and trustworthy, in the beginning it pays to cover all your bases and get someone who can independently advise you and does not have any ties to the franchise itself.

It is also important to understand that your accountant can only advise you and that it is up to you whether or not you will follow their recommendations. Keep in mind that these folks are financial experts and have knowledge far more diverse and specialized than you or I will likely ever have. But that is not to say that everyone is always right or infallible.

If you are given advice that you find strange or unreasonable, it might make sense to get a second opinion much like you would if your doctor told you that you needed surgery.

If that is the case, take your records and data and get a second opinion. Then, manned with even more information, make an informed decision that is right for you.

It is best to be more conservative at this point so that you be assured of having the money, or access to the money, that you may need over the next few months. Lines of credit that are available to you but never used cost you very little and can be a great resource to have when needed. But interest rates and other factors might make one source of funds a better deal over the long run. Your accountant will be able to advise you of that as well.

Whatever you do, never knowingly go into a new business without sufficient capital to see you through until the business becomes established. Nothing can be more frustrating than to have to close your business right before it starts to become profitable just because money ran out.

Money and finances are best when handled in a pro-active manner. That means planning ahead and understanding what is likely to happen in the upcoming months. While some things will almost always pop up when you least expect them, you will find yourself much better prepared when you have your financial house in order from day one.

While it is perfectly fine to have hopes and dreams, keep in mind that some of those hopes and dreams will require money and financing to turn them into realities. So pay attention to money and your finances. Have as much money up front as you can and keep financing and loans to a minimum. Pay attention to what your accountant says so that you can be reasonable assured of being able to start and grow a successful business.

Can You, and Will You, Follow Instructions?

Regardless of the franchise model you may choose, one thing will remain constant. That is the fact that you will have to follow their procedures, rules and regulations as you go about doing business under their franchise name. This is required to ensure a uniform brand experience from location to location.

For many people, this does not cause a problem as people appreciate when they are given a proven plan with specific instructions to follow. This usually results in much less work and far less planning and trial and error. Following something that has been proven over time is almost always better than trying to invent something new that would be as successful.

But for other people, following orders or procedures can be a daunting task. These people usually think they have a better or more productive way of doing things. Or they might figure that their choices of stock or products will do better than what is offered at the other franchise locations. Perhaps they might think that they have a better way of treating customers and growing their business.

While all of the above might very well be true, independent thinking, especially at the root level of the business, is frowned upon. That is because when you join a franchise, you are agreeing to provide the same type and level of services that all the other locations are providing to their customers. If you do something different, even though it could very well be better, it will provide a different level or type of service against which other franchise locations might be judged.

For example, if you purchase a burger franchise from one of the major fast food chains, you are expected to provide burgers with the same quality of meat and the same ingredients as everyone else. If you add or subtract ingredients, or if you make your burgers smaller or larger, you change the experience for the customer and that is something franchises are strongly against. We will cover this in more detail later.

The other reasons that franchises require their franchise owners to follow a specific business model and its set of procedures is that this model has been shown to work well in many different and diverse environments. Even though no business can have a cookie cutter approach to success, the main focus of the business model has been proven to be effective and profitable for the franchises and their owners.

So before you commit to purchasing a franchise, you should ask yourself if you are capable and willing to follow instructions and adhere to someone else's business plan. You also have to ask yourself whether you are going to be willing to follow the advice and direction of the franchise even if you feel you have a better way of doing things. If the answer to any of these questions is "no" or if you are not sure, franchising might not be the right option for you.

It is important for any franchise owner to understand that while a franchise is your own business, you do not have unilateral control or freedom to do whatever you please while under the franchise brand. Even though this is really a business that you own yourself, you are responsible for operating it in the same manner as all other franchise owners.

For this reason, you should discuss in detail exactly what you are supposed to do when it comes to operating your franchise location.

Get as much detail as possible to get an idea of what kind of restrictions you will have to operate under. If the restrictions are fair for the most part and you agree with them in principle, it might not be an issue for you.

But if you feel the restrictions are too intrusive and too confining, then perhaps you should either reconsider the brand you are looking at or perhaps abandoning the franchise concept all together.

This is important because if you don't follow the rules and procedures set in the contract you can be fined and even have your franchise license revoked without a refund of the amount you paid. So the end result is that you lose your business and any and all money or other resources you put into it to date.

As with any of the other decisions you will need to make, always be honest. If you have a hard time following orders that does not mean there is anything wrong with you. It just means that franchising might not be something that you are equipped to handle. If that is the case then you might be better off going it alone, even though that plan has a lot more risks associated with it.

If you were in the Armed Services, how did you like following orders and living in a rigid environment?

If you worked in a very structured corporate environment that was full of rules and guidelines and established procedures, how did you function in that environment? Did you find it confining or frustrating? Did you have problems doing things a certain way because you thought you had a better way?

Another option might be to get the experience you need in a franchise environment and once you get that business established, hire someone to run it for you, following all the required rules and procedures, while you go out and start your own business on your own. That way you will get the experience you need to be successful and then have a business you can grow and operate any way you see fit.

Most franchises have procedures in place for suggesting changes in the way franchises are run or changes to the product selection that is offered. Keep in mind that the goal of every franchise is to produce as much profit for as many locations as possible. A good franchise will listen to its owners and take their suggestions to heart. That might be something you ask other franchise owners as you ask them about their experiences before you sign on the dotted line.

As we will say often in this book, the more information you have available to you the better decisions you will be equipped to make.

What do you Like?

Usually people start businesses around something they either are knowledgeable about or enjoy very much. Many a business has been built from a hobby or other passion. People invent better products and services based on their own experiences and expertise and the results are often successful businesses and innovation.

The other reason for this is because since running your own business takes so much time and commitment, it just makes sense that you should do something you enjoy and have a passion for. This way your efforts and time are not really considered "work" but instead something you just enjoy doing.

Doing something you enjoy makes it easier to sacrifice your time and energy and direct it into your business. Long days don't seem quite so long when you are doing something you enjoy.

Working 7 days a week doing something you love is a lot easier than working 5 days a week doing something you hate. So all things considered, it makes sense to pick an industry and a business that you can relate to and enjoy.

Doing something we enjoy also allows us to remain more committed for longer periods of time. It gives us an increased ability to work through the tough or hard times because we believe in what we are doing and are enjoying the process. In other words, we are searching for ways to make our business work, not for ways to get away from it because we hate it.

Knowledge and expertise plays an important role in how successful we are as well. If I love my business and what I do chances are I will do whatever I can to learn more about it and the products I sell. I probably use some of the products as well and that enable me to serve my customers better.

When people come into my business with a question, chances are that I will have experienced the same thing or had the same questions. So I probably know the answers based on my knowledge and experience. That means my customers now have a place to come where they have a resource (Me!) that they can draw upon whenever they want. All because I am doing something I love.

In order to accomplish that you have to have some kind of skill or interest that is marketable or that lends itself to a particular type of business. Fortunately, just about everything we do lends itself to some form of already established business or industry. It is usually a short step from having a hobby to owning a business built around that hobby.

People who love to fish can open a bait shop or fishing store. People who love to cook can open a restaurant. People who love video games can open a video game store selling games and gaming systems and accessories. Even people who love to sleep all the time could own a store specializing in custom mattresses or pillows. If you enjoy doing something, trust me, there's a market for it.

The key is to discover the most successful and profitable market segment for your particular skills and things you enjoy. For example, if you like to take naps and eat hamburgers, one would think that opening your own hamburger restaurant would be the more profitable choice. But also keep in mind that a custom pillow or sleep center might work out well for you as well.

The main focus should be on avoiding the things in life you really don't like. If you hate pizza or Italian food, then opening a pizza place might be profitable in your area but you would hate every minute of it.

If you hate reading, a bookstore likely would be a poor choice for you as well. So you primary intent should be to find the type of business that fits you best. Once you have found your niche, then start exploring for the best and most attractive franchise opportunity.

Another factor to be considered when deciding on which type of franchise you should buy is what type of work is involved in running that franchise. If it is a service based franchise that provides services to the customer then you should be someone who enjoys direct contact with customers. If you are not that kind of person, then you either have to look for another type of business or hire people to interact with the customer freeing you up for other things.

As far as customer service is concerned, every business involves some form of customer service. After all, no business can possibly succeed without concentrating on customer service. Make your customers happy and they will come back. Anger them or treat them poorly and they will look elsewhere. But some businesses have different levels of direct customer contact so that might be a consideration for a prospective franchise owner.

The other reason for doing something you like is because, unless you start businesses with the idea of selling them for a profit later on, your business is a long term commitment.

While you might take a job you dislike because it is an important stepping stone in your efforts to get your dream job, starting your business is the exact opposite.

When you start your own business it is not usually a stepping stone. Instead of looking at your business as a way to get somewhere else, most business owners look for ways to make their businesses bigger and more profitable. So that means investing more of your time and efforts not less. That will be much easier if you will be doing something you enjoy and find fun.

When looking at a prospective franchise, consider what an average day will be like for you if you join that franchise. Will you be spending a lot of time doing what you love or will you be spending most of your time doing things you hate or have little interest in? That is a huge question that needs to be answered.

For one last powerful reason to choose something you love, think about your chances for success.

Success usually doesn't come to the person with the best new product or the best looking store. Long-term success comes to people who are committed to what they are doing and who are always looking for ways to make their businesses bigger and better and more responsive to their customer's needs. That takes knowledge, expertise and effort.

If you really find something you love, the odds that you will become successful are far greater than if you do something just for the money. Money is at best a temporary motivator. Eventually the novelty of the money wears off and you are confronted with the actual day to day activities that business owners have to take care of.

If those are the things you really enjoy, you will become very good at them. People will come to your store because you show then that you care about them and the products and services your business offers. People flock to service and information and great products more than they do for just the lowest price.

It has been said that the person who does what they really love will never have to work a single day in his or her life. Once you experience that you will understand exactly what that means.

Which Franchise is Right for You?

Hopefully you have done your research and a bit of soul searching and are now comfortable with going ahead and becoming a franchise owner. You have done your preliminary skills and attitude assessment and are familiar with what is going to be expected of you as you become a business owner. If you have not done any of these things I advise you to stop and do them now as this information is critical to your long term success and also in helping you pick the ideal franchise.

There are several factors that come into play when deciding on the best franchise for your particular situation. There are no franchises that are perfect for everyone and unfortunately, there are many differences between franchise models that can influence your decision on which one to choose.

I strongly urge you to have a financial planner or accountant in your employ at this point because only when you fully understand the financial commitments and requirements will you be able to make a reasonably accurate decision. Costs and financial commitments will vary widely among franchises so this is often one of the most important and critical factors to consider during your search.

With all of that being said, here are a few things you should consider when deciding which franchise is the best for you. These are only the high level things and you should not consider the list complete. Depending on your own area and situation, other factors might come into play. That is why it makes good sense to have others help you through this process and give you the benefit of their expertise. We are going to go over most of these items in detail in later chapters so for now this is just a short overview as it pertains to selecting your perfect franchise.

Size & Scope

Naturally everyone who goes into business wants to get the most customers and make the most money. After all, no one goes into business with the hopes of breaking even and just being able to pay the bills!

But when it comes to franchising, bigger is not always better. The larger and more established the franchise is, the higher the entrance fees and other fees are likely to be. That is simply because the brand name is stronger, more established and overall more valuable. While that is a good thing, in some cases it might not be worth the additional expense.

For example, if you live in a small town or a non metropolitan area where the lion's share of your business is going to come from local people and the people in surrounding towns, it might not be worth the additional expense to join a franchise that has a large national presence. The costs associated would be much higher and, unless you live in a popular vacation spot, you are not likely to get a significant percentage of your sales from people in other parts of the country.

For example, if you live in a small town in the Northeast, you may do just as well with a franchise that is primarily located in the Northeast and has brand recognition in the Northeast. Harry's Donuts, with 30 locations in the Northeast might be a good fit because most of the people in the Northeast will recognize Harry's Donuts. No one is California would recognize the brand but you won't get many people from California in your area so that is not much of an issue.

But the fees to join Harry's are going to be much less than a national donut franchise so you will save money and your sales will not be much less. The lesson here is to go with the franchise that offers you the best overall value for the area you are located in and the people that come to your business. Bigger is not always better but it will always be more expensive!

Costs and Fees

When anyone decides to start their own business, franchise or otherwise, the first thing they think of is money. How much will they need? What are the on-going costs? What are the monthly costs? How much profit can they expect? Does this make financial sense?

There are basically two sets of costs. Your initial investment in joining the franchise and getting the business off the ground. In additional you will have your recurring costs each month or year and that would include franchise fees, payroll, inventory, taxes and professional fees.

We should point out that any business you start is going to have fees attached to it. You cannot operate a business without paying some kind of expense to get it started and keep it running.

But with franchises you have an upfront fee to become an owner and this can be anywhere from tens of thousands of dollars to a million dollars or more for well known and established franchises. After that you have a franchise fee based on your sales or possibly even a fixed fee for on-going use of the brand.

When considering different types of franchises, consider only the ones that you honestly feel you can afford. Paying too much up front might keep you from keeping the business afloat during the first few months where businesses get established. As we have said before, insufficient capital is one of the most common reasons why new businesses fail.

Make sure your accountant is part of this process. They can help you accurately forecast how much you will need and for how long. The franchise owners themselves will also be able to help you forecast these costs as well.

Rules and Regulations

Every franchise system has its own business plan and rules and regulations. These rules and regulations must be followed and most of the time they must be followed to the letter.

As part of the franchise agreement, it will be stated that the franchisee agrees to these various rules and regulations and agrees to implement and follow them in their business.

This is important because there could be significant expense or time involved in adhering to their particular business plan. So before signing on the dotted line, make sure you understand exactly what is expected of you as you operate your franchise. If something isn't clear, ask specific and pointed questions. Don't be shy or take things for granted because failing to follow these rules and regulations could result in termination of your franchise and loss of your investment.

Restrictions

I must remind everyone that even though a franchise is your own business, the brand is not yours and the business model is not yours either. Your franchise fees include permission for your business to function under their name and to use their brand and carry their products.

Once you understand this, you will quickly see that there may be restrictions on what you can or cannot do in your franchise business. For example, one restriction might be that you have to buy everything, from products to cleaning supplies, from the franchise warehouse.

You would not have the ability to buy from other vendors even if you found their prices better or more competitive.

Depending on the specific franchise, they might have more or fewer restrictions placed on the franchisee. Keep in mind that the more restrictions that are in place the fewer options you will have in operating your business.

Too many restrictions might be a red flag and that is something you should be aware of. For example, if you have to use the franchise accountants and lawyers and have to have permission from the franchise owner to place small ads or run local promotions, then you might want to think twice about entering that agreement.

On the flip side, certain restrictions are necessary to insure consistent customer experience and overall franchise quality. For example, if you operate a franchise hamburger location, you must use the same burgers and fries from the same supplier or your food will be different from the other locations. But what cleaning products you use on your floors, or what toilet paper you use in your rest room is not that critical to the overall customer experience.

The ideal franchise arrangement allows the franchisee to run their own business with some degree of latitude while still assuring the rest of the franchise owners that the customer experience in every location will be identical to their location.

Type of Products and Services

When you consider a specific franchise, give careful thought as to the type of products and services they provide. Do not base your decision on the costs involved or the overall profitability. That could be a huge mistake.

You should have some knowledge about your products and services and it should be something that you have an interest and passion about. This is important so that you will enjoy your business and have an interest in spending the time you will need to spend to make it successful.

Also, make sure the products and services you will be selling are in demand in your particular area or location. We will go into more detail on this later but for now, stay away from franchises that offer products and services that do not align well with your location and the people around the area.

Logistics

The location of your franchise in relation to the franchise headquarters and other locations might be a consideration for some owners. Ideally franchises should not be all by themselves in a geographical area. If the nearest franchise location is 2,000 miles from the area that you want to open in, think about how easy or difficult it might be to get supplies and products delivered to you.

Also think about how often you would get support and how easy it would be to access the company when you need help or assistance.

Depending on the products you offer, it might not make economical sense to send a truck out to just one location. In these cases you might have to agree to minimum levels of purchases or risk widely spaced deliveries which might make replacing inventory a difficult process.

For example, let's say you are operating a burger franchise that is 3,000 miles away from the next nearest franchise location. Because of this, you will get deliveries only once every two weeks. You see approx. 10,000 burgers every two week so you stock 15,000 burgers to give you some flexibility.

But there is a big outdoor concert one weekend and you sell 13,000 burgers that weekend and now you have only 2,000 burgers available for the next week and a half. Because you are so far away, that might be a problem.

Cost of freight might be an issue as well and result in you paying more for product than other franchise owners. If this is a concern, make sure you have commitments in writing before making any kind of commitments.

Generally speaking, it is good to have other locations near you to give you an indication that this particular franchise would work in your area. But you should not have so many of the same type franchises in a small area that the population cannot sustain them all.

Training & Support

Part of the attractiveness of a franchise is the help and support you will be given especially in the early days of establishing and building your business. Ask what kind of support you will receive as part of your franchise fees.

Will you have a local support rep assigned to your location that will visit you regularly to give you an update on how you are doing compared to other locations? Is there training before your business opens so that you can hit the ground running as soon as your doors are opened? Can you work in a franchise for a few weeks to get the feel of things so you will be confident when your business opens?

Training and support is a big part of owning and operating a franchise. If this is missing or weak, that should be an area of concern. As with anything else, ask specific questions and get everything in writing.

Industry Stability and Viability

Even the best franchise today might fail tomorrow if it doesn't adapt with the marketplace. That means constantly updating the products and services they provide to keep everything current. If the franchise doesn't do that, it will fail. For anyone who doesn't think this is important, I need only remind everyone of all the video stores in the 1980's. There was one on every corner and now there are either very few or none what so ever.

Ideally you should pick a franchise where the market is growing but not brand new. It should be established to cut down on the risk but still have a lot of growth t give you time to get into the market and survive.

Also, when thinking about a franchise think of longevity. No one wants to go into business, have a good first year, and then go out of business because the market no longer exists. While there are some models in which this can work, it is a lot of work with a lot of risk. This requires specialized knowledge, a huge support team, and time to get things done extremely fast to take advantage of the local fads and market trends. This does not usually lend itself to franchise opportunities.

Your Area

I cannot impress on you the importance of knowing your area where your new franchise will be located.

The products and services must match the population and their needs. You can sell a lot of hay in an area where there are a lot of farms but you won't sell very much in a metropolitan area. We will go into more detail on this later.

Choosing the perfect franchise for you is likely going to hinge on more than one factor. There will be good and bad points with every franchise. Some of the bad points, such as fees required, might be outright deal breakers while other would be relatively minor. They key is maintaining everything in perspective and having the most information available to you before making your decision.

This is usually not a black and white process. Everything will have its own level of importance and you should take those into consideration. So instead of good and bad, try and include importance in the equation as well. Consider a point system of 1 to 5 or 1 to 10. Then, you can rank factors according to importance as well and positive or negative.

For example, if the franchise fee is $500,000 and you ultimate limit is $200,000, than that would be a negative 10 on your list which would indicate a deal breaker. But if the fee was $210,000 and your ideal limit was $200,000 that might be a negative 2 or 3. That means it is a negative but not something that would necessarily keep you from moving ahead if everything were equal.

The key to choosing the right franchise is going into the process with your eyes wide open and being totally honest with yourself and what you want and need from your business. The more information you have at your disposal, the more accurate your decision will ultimately be.

Do not rush through this process. The more time you spend investigating and researching now the better decision you will make at the end. This means fewer mistakes, an overall better fit, and a great chance of achieving success in your new business. We will be discussing other things you can do to help you decide in future chapters.

Franchise Discovery Days & Research

Hopefully by this time we have determined what kind of Franchise we want to open and hopefully narrowed it down to a few of what we consider the best ones available in our area. The next step is to take our research one step further and do a little investigating.

There is no better way to learn about any business than actually going in and seeing a few locations in person. See the building, see how it feels to you and get a first-hand look at the products and services they offer.

Interact with the people behind the counter and see how their treat their customers. Notice how you feel as you walk through the store and make a purchase. Is the experience positive? Did you feel like you would want to come back in the future?

Or does the store not impress you and the experience leave a lot to be desired? These are some of the things that you cannot read about in any book or manual.

Try and do this at several locations. Even if it takes you a few days and a couple of hundred miles on your car. Take some friends or your wife and make an adventure out of it. Get a feel for as many locations as you possibly can. Remember these are individually owned operations and even though they have the same name and follow the same business plan, there will be subtle differences between locations. So don't base your opinion on just one location.

If you have made inquires with the franchise about joining, don't go just to the locations they give you. Chances are they will send you to the best and most impressive locations because they want to look as good as they possibly can in your eyes. Instead, go to a couple of those locations and then a few in other areas. In fact, if there are a few "seedy" areas near where you want to open your business, visit a location or two there if they exist. If the locations in those areas are impressive, that is a good sign.

I also advise you to talk to a few of the employees and the owners themselves if they are available. Very often employees will give you more honest answers about what it is like working for that franchise.

This will give you insights into whether you are going to have trouble keeping employees happy and whether or not employee turnover will be a problem.

Talk to the owners and the manager and explain to them that you are thinking about joining as a new franchisee. Ask them what they think of the company and how they are to work for. Keep in mind that they might be hesitant to be totally honest in fear of word getting back to the company itself regarding their comments. That is why employees tend to be more honest than owners.

Perhaps the best way to get first-hand knowledge of what operating a franchise is like is by attending an open house or "Discovery Day" that is sponsored by the franchise operation.

During this event, people get to see first-hand what the franchise is actually like. They get tours of the facility, access to the inner workings of the franchise and the ability to speak to people who are actually doing what they are considering.

These events will give you a sense of what is involved and what it would be like to spend day after day running the franchise. This gives you a far better idea than reading about it in a book or watching a video or PowerPoint presentation. Actually seeing and experiencing thins is often the best and most accurate way of learning and evaluating something.

Keep in mind, however, that these events are being sponsored and held by the franchise itself. So you are going to meet the most successful people and talk to the most positive owners. You are going to hear the most positive success stories and the very best things about the franchise. You are not going to get the full story. But just the fact that you will have the ability to experience things first hand is important.

You will also begin to see if you "fit in" with other franchise owners and how they view their businesses. If you are in a room with 50 serious minded people dressed in 3 piece suits and you are a happy go lucky guy who prefers jeans and t-shirts, you might not fit in that well. It doesn't make you less of a person or less of a businessman. It just means you are different than everyone else and you might be judged because of it.

Almost all industries and market segments will have more than one franchise operating within it. Attend a few of these "discovery days" and get a feel for each franchise. Try and see which one you feel the most comfortable with and which one is the best fit for you. You might think one is perfect until you compare it to another and find the second one is actually the better fit.

Whether you go to one or 20 of these events, always be honest and have an open mind. Ask questions and be honest about what you are looking for and what you are prepared to give to your business.

It is better to find out about any potential problems or issues now instead of later.

These days might be your only opportunity to ask questions to a wide range of people at the same time. It also is a good idea to pay close attention to the questions asked by the other attendees as well. Most of the time people will ask a question that many other people wonder about but are afraid to ask. Keep your eyes and ears open and take notes. Make note of any answers that might appear evasive or questions where the franchise people try and immediately change the subject to something else. This can highlight potential problem areas they do not want you to know about.

When you visit other locations, try and get a feel for the areas they operate in and try and match those areas with the area you are considering. This can be an important factor is judging suitability. Do not compare rural locations with city locations. The data will probably be misleading.

Legal Matters

Disclaimer: I am not a lawyer and neither are the publishers or sellers of this book. This chapter is not intended to dispatch legal advice and should not be used in that fashion. Your legal situation will vary from person to person and should always be discussed with a licensed attorney who is familiar with you, your business and your individual situation.

As with any business or major purchase, everyone should have competent legal representation before making any decisions or signing any agreement or contract. This is necessary because the average person like you and I cannot hope to be able to even begin to understand the legal language contained in every contract or paper.

What might seem innocent and trivial in a contract may very well commit you to something very expensive or significant down the road. The contract or agreement might contain language and content so one-sided and biased towards the other party it would be harmful for you to sign it in the first place.

But without someone to step in and read the contracts and documents and give us their opinion of them based on their content as the law sees it, we may soon enter into something we would seriously regret later. Since that is something we usually would prefer to avoid, having good legal representation is important.

My advice to anyone who is thinking about starting their own business of any kind is to seek out a lawyer experienced in business and contract law. This is a specific branch of law and you would be wise to get a lawyer with that particular type of experience. Make sure you get a lawyer that is licensed to practice in the state in which you register your business in case problems should arise.

Have your lawyer be involved from the very beginning. As you do your research and decide on the business or franchise you like the best, have them review the contracts and other information from the franchise and have them investigate the company as well. This will help you protect yourself against making a bad investment with a company with legal problems or a rash of lawsuits against them.

When you are ready to join the franchise, have your lawyer involved every step of the way.

Have them review and approve the contracts, make any required changes to better protect you and your business, and to make sure the contracts are fair and reasonable for everyone concerned.

Your lawyer can also help you with such things as incorporating your business, creating a DBA (a "Doing Business As" name for your business) or filing assorted paperwork for permits and other state and local requirements.

Hiring a good lawyer can be expensive but most attorneys will be more reasonable with a new start-up business as they will see the opportunity for long-term business from the account. In any case, a good lawyer, with a good reputation is not going to come cheap. But regardless of the price, they are an absolute necessity when it comes to starting your own business.

Sometimes the franchise itself will recommend or offer to provide you with a lawyer to handle the entire process for you. I would advise against this because there is a possibility of a conflict of interest. That means the lawyer has interests on both sides of the process. They are getting referrals from the franchise and payment from you. So it might be the lawyer will not have your total best interests at heart. They want to make the franchise happy so they keep sending referrals so that might tend to alter their views as far as your situation is concerned.

There are a few ways that you can find a good lawyer. You can contact the State Bar Association and they will ask you what kind of lawyer you need and will recommend someone in your area. You can check the local ads or Yellow Pages but I would do that only as a last resort. The very best way is to use someone recommended by someone you know who has that particular type of lawyer for their business.

Most lawyers will offer a free consultation with new clients. During this consultation you can sit down and talk with the lawyer and get a feel for the type of person he is and decide how well the two of you will work together. There really should be a certain comfort level between you and your lawyer because you will have to work together closely in the future.

You can also use this opportunity to discuss your business and what your legal needs might be. While you will have a pretty good idea before the consultation, I almost guarantee you will discover one or two things you hadn't thought of. Which is exactly why you should have a lawyer in the first place!

You might want to meet a couple of lawyers and then make your decision on which one is the best fit for you. Personality, skills and experience are all important factors that should be considered before deciding on the right lawyer for you.

Do not gloss over this and pick the first name in the Yellow Pages or settle for the lawyer the franchise uses. This is your money and future at stake so time spent now will help you a great deal later.

In some cases, you might find a lawyer who is also an accountant. Many financial advisors have this dual specialty so you might be able to get two resources from the same person. That way the lawyer can look at things from both a legal and financial perspective at the same time. This could prove valuable for you. But be careful and make sure that this person is acting as a lawyer as well and will be available to represent you in legal situations as the need arises.

Speaking of representation, trust me, you will need it eventually. We live in a lawsuit dominated world right now and indications are that it is only going to get worse before it gets better. People sue for all kinds of reasons and many of those reasons make no sense whatsoever. But those situations still require representation and you will need a lawyer on your side to protect your interests.

You would also need an attorney to draw up papers for incorporation and to protect your private possessions and interest from your business liabilities. That is why a lawyer fully experienced in business law is your best choice.

It is not a question of whether you need a lawyer or not. It is a question of when you will need one. The answer to that question is that you need a lawyer NOW rather than later.

Know Your Industry

Before starting any business, it is critical that you fully understand the industry or market for that type of business. Chances are you will be risking or dedicating significant financial resources to your new business and you should expect a reasonable chance of success for risking those resources.

Your business should meet a few important criteria before you even consider opening your business. While the following list is not all inclusive, it is a good start. Keep in mind there may be more things for you to consider based on your own particular location and business type.

Age of Market

Is the market that you are going to enter a stable market, just beginning or a long running market? Each type of market has its own advantages or disadvantages and these can significantly influence your ability to start a profitable business.

It is important to understand this because a new market will be riskier but possibly have a greater reward. The market itself might sound good but has not been proven yet. So you might make a real killing or you could lose everything. The good news is that brand new markets are usually cheaper to enter and are less competitive. Franchises in new markets are somewhat rare and therefore have lower entry fees.

A stable market will be less risky as it has already proven itself but might be more competitive and more expensive to enter. This means that others have started similar businesses and have done quite well. But that also means that you will be going head to head with more established business and that can make things tough in the beginning. Franchises in a stable market are more expensive because they have a proven track record and are considered less risky.

A long running market might be already on the downside or be over saturated and that might make it more difficult for a newcomer to enter the market and have a decent shot at becoming profitable. Long running markets can be a good choice if you are confident that the products and services are well suited for the future as well as the present. Otherwise, see the next item.....

Future of the Market

Many products have a life cycle and if your business is based on just one product or type of product that could mean your business will also have a limited life as well. So you should be aware of the type of product you sell and try to envision and predict where that product will be 10 or 20 years from now.

Remember the corner video stores in the 1980's? They were all over and franchises were popping up all over the place. Now there are any left as automated machines are dispensing DVD's for a buck a day! No one would make a dime in a videotape store these days.

If your product or industry is deemed a limited time product, that doesn't mean there is not money to be made. People can make a ton of money for a limited time and then just move on to the next limited time product. But you need to understand this going into the business and not discover this after investing a ton of money into a business that has only a year or two left on its product cycle.

Competition within the Market

In any market, there are only a limited number of customers with a limited amount of need. If there are too many stores or businesses selling the same product, there will not be enough demand to sustain all those businesses.

When this happens, only the stronger or most established businesses will remain while the others will be forced to close.

For example, a town might be able to support 3 hamburger restaurant and give their owner's a nice living. But if 15 burger places opened up, there would not be enough demand and some would fail. This is the same in any industry. The market has to be able to support the businesses within the market in order for everyone to be successful.

Also, the "big boys" or the largest stores with the best reputation, lowest prices and higher brand recognition are going to capture the largest market share. If there are a lot of similar businesses, or a few big boys in your market, that is something you should consider very carefully.

Market Penetration

Are there other similar businesses in your particular market in your area? If there are, then you need to consider whether or not the market is already saturated or not. If there are no similar businesses, this might be a great thing or a bad thing.

Businesses are located where they can be successful. You would not see a skate park in a retirement community or a hamburger restaurant in a vegetarian community. It is just not a good fit.

So if you don't see any similar type businesses in your area of choice, you need to ask yourself why. Maybe no one has tried and the area is begging for the first or maybe people have tried in the past and there was just no market for that particular product or service. You really need to do your research before committing resources to a business that is not already in that area.

Demographics

Just as important, in fact sometimes even more important, are the people in the area that your business is going to be located in. If you are selling online, then location isn't as important as what your customers want and how many of those people will want your particular product or service.

For this book we are concentrating on franchise businesses which are primarily brick and mortar stores that may also sell on line. But for any business to succeed, we must have people who want our products accessible to us.

The ideal business would be located in an area chocked full of people who desperately need their product. A prime example of this would be utilities. People need water and electricity and they have to have somewhere to purchase it. Even if they don't want it, they NEED it. So the power company is bound to be successful.

People need food so if you open the only supermarket in town, you would probably be successful as well. If your area is primarily populated by senior citizens then any business that sells products targeted towards seniors would probably do well, too. The key is to know what type of people are in your area and what they need or want. If your business sells those products, you have a good match. If not, then it is best to look for a new business or a new location.

Product Need Lifespan

Another aspect of demographics involves how long people will have a need for your product. People with children will only purchase toys until their children get to be a certain age and then their purchases will transition into other items. A perfect example of this would be diapers. Parents need diapers for only a few years and then they will start buying underwear instead.

Limited lifespan products require a constantly changing population in order to sustain sales or grow market share. So you either have to pick an area with this kind of population growth or change or develop other products to sustain sales. Either way, you have to factor is lifespan and demand into your business model unless you sell products that people will always need such as food, transportation and clothing.

Logistics

Logistics is the process by which you get products to and from your location. Ideally your business should be easy to get to and have easy and fast access to products, supplies and customers.

If your customers have to travel a long ways to get to your business, chances are they will look for another alternative. If it is costly or difficult to get products and supplies to your business then you will not be able to offer competitive pricing or a responsive business to your customers.

For businesses in large metropolitan areas this is usually not a concern. But for rural businesses, or for those franchise locations that are far away from other locations, this could be a serious problem.

Seasonal or Year Round?

Last, but certainly not least, is understanding how demand for your products and services will translate into sales throughout the year. There are some businesses and locations that are seasonal in nature. For example, you will sell a lot of ice cream in July and August but very little in January and February. Resort areas that are teeming with people in the summer might be totally shut down and vacant during the winter.

For seasonal businesses you have to determine if the sales you make during your busier parts of the year are enough to sustain the business for the rest of the year. If you make $30,000 in three months and nothing for the rest of the year you make $30,000 a year. Bills and taxes come in every month but sales for only a few months. You need to understand if it is realistic to own that type of business or a business in that area.

The advantage of a seasonal business is that you can work hard for 3 months and then relax for the other months if the sales were high enough. Or, some people own two businesses that are open during opposite times of the year and move from location to location for the busy times of each area.

All of these items have one important thing in common. That is that you need to understand every one of these things BEFORE you commit to starting a particular business. It makes little sense to open the business first and then start thinking about these things.

But even after you open a business, you should keep all of these things in mind, as well as other factors that pertain to your business or area so that you can spot new trends and become aware of shifts that occur within your marketplace.

Very few things stay the same in this world. But in business, if you are successful, people will see that and try to enter your market and share in that success. What was a vibrant business today could be shut down tomorrow if the competition changes and the business owner is not aware of it until it is too late.

Never has the phrase "knowledge is power" or "knowledge is money" been truer when it comes to understanding your market and the people within it. Always be aware of everything as it pertains to your marketplace so that you can react to changes and know when it is smart or foolish to enter or remain in a particular market or location.

Product Availability

We will actually cover this in two areas in this publication. For this section, we need to understand who makes the products or provides the services for what you will be selling in your industry. If the franchise does not actually manufacture or directly provide the products and services, who does?

This is important because the entire franchise model might be dependent on the work or products manufactured by others. So if that company should go bankrupt, or get into a disagreement with the franchise home office, everyone could be negatively affected.

If the source for the products or services goes away, what will happen to your business? This can be a real concern and you should make sure you understand this completely.

This is not to say that a successful franchise must make or provide their own products or services in order to be successful and a good opportunity. After all supermarkets and convenience stores sell products made by major manufacturers. But that is different because these products usually are available from several different distributors. It is when a product or service is only available from one or two sources that this can become problematic.

Know Your Products

Before you decide on which franchise you are going to join, you need to understand the products and the market for those products. Just like you wouldn't buy a house without looking at the neighborhood and having an engineer look it over, neither should you commit to a business without understanding what their products have to offer and who buys them.

With some types of franchises understanding the products is easy. Burger franchises sell food, oil change franchises sell convenience and maintenance services that appeal to drivers and car owners and convenience stores sell coffee, soft drinks, fast food and other items that people can just run in and get in minutes. All these franchise sell convenience. In other words, you can get what you want and you can get it fast. That's pretty easy to understand.

But they key is understanding the overall appeal of the product. The broader the appeal the easier it is going to be to make sales and earn income. For example, if you have the choice of two products and when everything else is equal, it is better to have a product that 50% of the people in an area buy instead of the product that only 20% of the people will buy. The more people who want the more of the product you will sell. That isn't rocket science.

That means that the more specific the use or application of a product is, the fewer people will likely use it. For example, everyone needs to eat so most everyone has gone to a burger place for a quick bite. Plus, the kids love those places and they pester their parents to take them there when it comes time to eat. So a fast food franchise would have a large number of people who want or need to use the products they are selling. No franchise can guarantee sales or success but this broad a product appeal is a really good thing to have on your side.

But let's say there is also a franchise for automobile painting and body work. While there are people who will need or want these services from time to time, the appeal of that product is nowhere near as great when compared to the burger franchise. After all, everyone needs to eat a couple of times a day but you might only need an auto painted once or twice in your lifetime.

This does not mean you can't make money with the painting franchise, it just means there is a broader product appeal to the food based item. But other things will factor in as well. There might be 47 burger places in your town but no auto painters. So one market might be saturated and the other one completely open.

Generally speaking, the broader the product appeal and the stronger the brand performance the more expensive the franchise will cost. This just makes sense because the more valuable franchise with the broadest appeal is worth much more and will generate larger income and profits for the owner.

So when you are looking for the best value and fit for you when it comes to franchises, ask yourself the following questions when it comes to the products you will be selling:

What Kind of Expertise or Knowledge Do You Have About the Products?

If you are going to sell something, you have to understand what the product is, what it does, what purpose the product has and why people are buying it. IN other words, you need to understand what the product does, why people need it, and how the product does it.

You will need this knowledge to advise customers on which product is the best one for them and how to make sure every customer makes the perfect buying decision. If the customer buys the wrong product, he is going to be unhappy and that is never good for both the customer and the business.

What About the Product do People Really Like?

Every popular product has at least one thing people really like about it. It might be the way it looks, it might be the price point, it might be more reliable, or it might do the job better than any other product out there.

People buy things because they feel a level of connection and security with that product. They might believe in the name and associate the name with quality or they just might buy it because they heard the name before. Perhaps they had bought the same product years ago and are looking for another because it did a great job and never broke down.

Understanding why people like a particular product makes it easier to sell and makes it easier to decide which products or businesses to be associated with. Since brand recognition is one of the prime advantages of purchasing a franchise, you should be aware of how your customers feel about brand recognition in the first place!

What Need or Problem Do Your Products Address?

People buy things because they like them or because they make life easier, better or more rewarding. You need to understand what every product does and how it does it so you will be more able to let the customer know all the things the product can do for them.

Customers will ask you how something works and you best be able to tell them. Don't think you can make something up either because your customer will see through that very quickly. When you start selling a product, you had better know that product inside out and better than any customer.

Is the Product Offering Something that You Feel Will Sell Well in Your Area?

Snow shoes will sell well in Alaska and Siberia but not all that well in Florida. Just because a products sells well in one area or location does not translate into guaranteed sales in another area.

The same would go to hang gliding equipment in a retirement village or scuba gear in the Sahara Dessert. Always make sure the product fits the area and the people who live in it. Not everything sells everywhere and to everyone.

How to the Costs Compare with Similar Products Sold Elsewhere?

A LOT of people are cost driven these days so it is important to understand where the franchise prices fall within the other sources for the same product in your area. While quality and other factors are important, price is usually one of the first criteria before a customer even walks through the door. They might wind up paying more somewhere else once quality is explained to them but at that point, you may already have lost a sale.

For example, if you sell hot dogs and your hot dogs are super high quality but sell for twice the price of other hot dogs in the area, people might never even try one because they might be scared away by the higher prices.

Your prices should be competitive with other retailers of the same or similar products. You can sell more expensive alternatives but you need to have competitively priced products to bring customers through your doors.

Are There Other Stores Selling Better Quality Products in the Area?

We said it before and we will say it again. If there are other businesses selling the same products in your area that can be both good and bad news.

It is good news because if there are successful businesses selling the same products for a long time it means there is a market for those products in your area.

But if there are too many businesses selling the same product you might have a hard time getting established in your area. But if your products are better or higher quality or do more things than your competitors, then you need to understand that and market your products accordingly.

Never think your customers will understand or recognize these differences. You need to take them by the hand and point out those differences to them. Sometimes you have to hit them over the head until they understand!

Using a combination of targeted marketing and exceptional product knowledge will help you not only establish your business but help it grow at the same time. If there is a lot of competition in your market you will need any advantage you possibly can get. Especially when you are the "new kid on the block". Once you get established and have a great reputation it will become easier to get sales. But in the beginning, you need to know everything about your products in order to market and present them effectively.

Is the Product Stable and Readily Available?

In order to sell products and services you have to have them to sell. That means you have to have easy access to the products and materials you use or sell. If access to what you need is difficult or extremely limited, that could represent a problem.

When evaluating potential franchises ask them where they get their product from and how long have they been doing business with those suppliers. Evaluate each product and determine how easy it would be to replace a current vendor with a new one. This will protect your business from the failure of a supplier or other problems that could result in an interruption of delivery.

Diversified Product Offerings

There is a saying in the financial world that goes "You don't put all your eggs in one basket". That refers to investing all your money in one place or with one company. The idea is that if that company should go bankrupt or lose value, your entire financial worth would not go along with it. You would have money invested elsewhere that would help defray other losses.

The same holds true for the products and services that your franchise delivers.

Ideally the franchise business you purchase should have more than one product or one group of products. There should be other products and services that appeal to different needs and/or different customers. That way as the demand or need for one product goes up or down, your entire business will remain more stable over time.

In addition, similar or complimentary products offer an ability to increase each individual sale. Most franchises have products that compliment other products. People do not buy just a burger; they will buy an order of fries or a soft drink or coffee too. So the $3 sale turns into a $6 sale, all from the same customer.

But the strength of having multiple and diversified products lies in the ability to replace one product for another as the demand changes. For example, let's say you rented video tapes in your video store and you never went along with the trend to DVD's. Gradually your customers who wanted DVD's would go somewhere else and your sales would dwindle until they stopped all together. But had you offered both video tapes and DVD's as they became more popular your customers would have still been able to get what they wanted and needed from your store.

Almost every store has products that used to be best sellers and now sell only a few units a year. But at the same time they introduced new products that only sold a few units at first but are now their best sellers.

When it comes to deciding which franchise to go with, look at the total product offering and see how well it provides for today's needs and also addresses the newest product trends as well.

If the franchise only sells one type of product, ask yourself what the future of that one product is. If it is not rock solid, then start thinking about another business.

Another reason for product diversification is having more products that will suit more customers. Just as you never see a restaurant that offers just one entrée, you should never tie the future of your business to just one particular product. You want enough products so that you have a product that suits just about anyone.

Even the burger places also have chicken sandwiches and salads. They don't do this because they like to. They do it because that is what their customers want. They want to attract groups and families who want to go to a place that has something for every appetite. Burgers for the kids, chicken for the Moms and Dads who want a healthier alternative and salads for those customers who are watching their weight and calories.

Ask to see what products the franchise has introduced since its inception. See how responsive they were to current trends and changes in the market. If they regularly introduced new products to replace poor sellers that is a good sign. If they are still offering the same products they were 50 years ago but they are well diversified and sell well, that might not be so bad,

But if they haven't changed their product offerings and sales have gradually declined over the years and they have done nothing to stop that trend, then you have something to be concerned about.

When it comes to product diversification, ask our self the following questions about the products a franchise will allow you to sell:

Are There Enough Products

Very few businesses can survive on one product. Your most successful businesses will have more than one type of product or several variations / quality levels of products for their customers to choose from. If there is only one or two products available, that can leave your business vulnerable to market change and for losing customers to other similar businesses that offer more choices to their customers.

Is There Something for Almost Everybody?

Successful businesses want people to come into their store and not their competition. That means making their product selection the most complete and the most attractive to wider range of people. If more people can find something they like at your business, more people will walk through your doors instead of the competition.

Are their Anchor Products and Upsell Products?

The most successful business models will have complementary products that customers can purchase at the same time as their primary purchase. For example, if you sell electronics you should also sell cables, accessories, cases, power supplies, blank discs and other items people are also looking to buy.

If you sell a product that requires other products in order to make it work, then you should offer those products as well. The classic example is selling batteries if you sell kids toys. People need them to make the toy work so they will have to buy them somewhere. It might as well be at your store!

Depending on the type of products you sell, consider having an upgraded or heavier duty model that costs a little more. For example, if you sell burgers sell a quarter pounder, a third pounder and possibly even a half pounder. If you sell cameras, have small camera, less expensive cameras as well as more expensive and professional cameras. Have a wide selection not only allows you to make more sales and more money, it also allows you to fit the customer with the best product for their needs. Then end result is a happier customer and more money in your pocket.

Are There Older Products and Newer Products?

Most well run franchises will have a mix between older and more established products and newer cutting edge products in their product line. This allows you to have stable selling products for your business to depend on while at the same time integrating new products which will eventually gain popularity and become tomorrow's best sellers.

If the franchise you are looking at has not changed their product line over the years that is something you should really look into. Maybe their products or services are as good today as they were 30 years ago. If that is the case, then it is no problem.

But most businesses eventually have to change their product lines when their once popular products stop selling. It is always best to be out in front of this than be forced to play catch-up.

How Responsive to Market and Industry Trends is the Franchise?

If you are planning to start a business in a particular market, then you probably have some knowledge of that product and market. Perhaps you worked in that business all your life and have a wealth of experience that you want to put to work for you in your own business.

If that is the case then you should have a pretty good idea of how well the franchise has kept up with the market over the last 10 years or so. If they have always been on the forefront of new products and services, that is a good thing. But if they always have lagged behind and introduced new things only because they had to, that is an attitude that I would be wary of.

Are There Regional Products Available?

There are some franchises that are in all different areas of the country and in countries all over the world. It might shock you to know that the product offering in one country might vary widely from the product offerings in another country. That is because the people and culture of that country require different products.

This might not apply to the industry or market you are interested in but if it does, inquire about whether or not the franchise has a choice of products based on culture or ethnicity. These might do very well in your area if you have a lot of people of a certain culture living in that area.

Are Franchisees Allowed to Add Products Based on Their Area?

Sometimes franchises are very strict about what you can sell and what you can't sell.

Other might allow you to add local favorites or regional based products to your product list if they sell well in your area.

But always be aware that the products must fit in with the overall brand and purpose of the franchise and cannot negatively affect the brand name or reputation. If this is a concern to you, or if adding additional products is something you would like the ability to do in your location, make sure to discuss this before commitment and get any answer clearly stated in writing.

What are the Costs Involved in Owning the Franchise?

It is almost impossible to start any business without some capital outlay of funds. Regardless of what type of format business you might be interested in, there will always be costs associated with it. But when you purchase a franchise, there are going to be additional charges involved and you need to be aware of these charges before making any commitment.

Keep in mind that these costs will vary greatly depending on location and how the business is to be started. If you are using an existing building that is already set up for your type of business, the time frame might be less. But if you are building your own building, it will take months, possibly a year or more, until you are ready for business.

Meanwhile costs will be incurred and no revenue will be coming in to offset these costs. So it is critical that you not only have the money to pay these costs and fees but also have the money to sustain the business until it is ready to open and then until it becomes profitable.

While the list below contains all the major or most common charges, there may be others involved with your specific franchise choice or the area in which your business is located in. So make sure you have a full understanding of what costs are going to be involved so you can determine whether or not you have the financial resources to take this business from an idea to an established and profitable business.

Initial Franchise Fee

When you go into a franchised business, you will have to pay an entrance fee to the parent company of the franchise. This fee allows you to do business under their brand name and other rights that will be detailed in the franchise contract.

This fee might be a few thousand dollars or a few hundred thousand dollars or more depending on the size and type of franchise you decide on. Generally the franchises with the largest number of locations and the strongest or most popular brand names will be the most expensive.

Keep in mind that the more popular the franchise and the stronger the brand image is will help determine how fast your business turns a profit and how successful it ultimately will become. It is up to you and your lawyer and accountant whether the larger entrance fees are appropriate for you and your situation. Bigger is not always better if you cannot afford it.

Building & Construction Fees

You have to have someplace to do business from and you will either be paying rent or building your own building on property that you own. Regardless of whether you rent or own there will be costs associated with your building and property.

If you build your own building on your own property there will also be the cost of land surveys, installation of utilities and architects fees. All of these are incurred before the first cement is poured or the first brick is set.

Your franchise may also have existing and established locations available for purchase as well. These will be more expensive but the lure of this is that you are ready to turn a profit immediately because your business is already up and running. This will be the closest thing to a turn-key business as possible.

Licenses Permits, Taxes

Franchise fees usually do not included property taxes, licenses, permits or any other form of government or regulatory requirements. For example, if you purchase a franchised restaurant you will still have to the costs to obtain a liquor license, food service permits and the insurance required under law for you to open the doors and serve the public.

Also not included would be property taxes, income taxes, payroll costs and their associated taxes and other similar expenses. These can add up quickly so make sure you and your account get a full disclosure on all these costs up-front.

Ongoing Royalties

Most franchises will have some kind of on-going monthly, quarterly or yearly fees. These fees might be fixed payments or payments based on actual sales. Make sure it is clearly spelled out o the franchise contract what these fees are to be and whether or not they are subject to increases later on.

These fees can be substantial and you should factor these in when it comes to determining what sales level you will need to make a profit. If fees are tied to profits that might be better for you in the beginning when sales are lower.

In any case, be very clear on when the fees start and when they are due. For example, if you sign up on January 1st but your business will not open until October 1st, when will the fees begin? Will they start in January or October? It's all in the language used in the contract. This is one example of why we need a lawyer before we sign on the dotted line!

Grand Opening Fees

Sometimes the franchise parent company will charge a grand opening fee to cover extra promotion and operating costs for a big grand opening event. There might be specific advertising and corporate presence involved as well as additional support to help make sure your business gets off the ground in a very positive manner.

If your franchise does charge this type of fee make sure you understand what is included and make sure you get everything you are entitled to. Understand that it is very important for your business to make the best impression possible from day one. Sometimes you only get one chance to impress a customer so doing things right is the best way to go.

Advertising Fees

Advertising fees are sometimes charged to each franchisee to cover regional and national advertising campaigns. While advertising can be expensive, when the costs are split between many different franchisees, you can get more advertising for less money.

If you are being charged this fee make sure to understand what kind of advertising this fee includes, where the advertising is to take place, the frequency and also the ability to see the advertising content in advance and approve it.

Also make sure that you have the right to accept or decline to participate in any special promotions the company decides to run. Sometimes this is not necessarily the case but you should be aware of what your commitments and obligations are as far as advertising is concerned.

Payroll Costs

Depending on the size of your business and how long it is open for business each day payroll may be a minor cost or a major expense. Some businesses are one or two man operations and can be staffed by just a few people. Other businesses that require many employees will require a much higher payroll.

Find out what the franchise recommends, or even requires, you to have as far as payroll is concerned.

Don't think for a minute that you will be able to be there 20 hours a day 7 days a week. Not only is that not reasonable, you would get burned out pretty quick and you might even have a few sick days thrown in there once in a while as well.

Figure on a reasonable payroll with yourself putting in some hours and then adjust your payroll up or down as the business grows. Your ideal payroll should provide you with adequate coverage at all times the business is open while enabling employees to provide a high level of customer service with minimal wait time.

Initial Inventory

Sometimes the franchise fee will include the costs of a starter inventory. This should be spelled out in detail in your franchise contract. Regardless of who pays for it, your business will need an initial stock or products to sell to customers. You will also need enough stock to re-stock the shelves until replacements are ordered and arrive

For example, if it takes 2 weeks from the time your order is submitted until it arrives at your front door you will need to have at least 2-3 weeks of stock on hand to cover the sales during that time frame. As your business becomes established, the sales coming in will pay for the replacement orders.

But at the beginning, there will be out of pocket costs for these materials and products.

Theft & Damage

Yes, unfortunately there will be on-going costs for theft and damaged products. Depending on your products being sold, you can count on a certain percentage of them walking out the door without being paid for. All businesses incur these costs to the extent that these costs are built into the retail prices. Your franchise should be able to give you the percentage of theft losses you can expect every month.

Also there will be costs for either franchise mandated or government mandated security cameras or other security related systems. Check with the franchise and the local codes and law enforcement to see what is required at your location.

In addition, you will have damage losses and other losses. A customer might knock something off a shelf, or something might fall from the shelves by accident. These things happen all the time and while you can take steps to minimize them, you cannot eliminate them.

As we said in the beginning, these are some of the most common fees involved with owning a franchise or regular type of business.

We did not include this information in order to scare you away from owning your own business. Instead, we wanted to make sure you were aware of these fees and costs so that you could make an informed decision on whether you can afford to go into business at this time or not.

So many people think that once they pay the hefty franchise fee they are home free and good to go. That is simply not true and it is best you know that now instead of when it is too late. In some cases, that franchise fee, even though it could be steep, is just the beginning of the bills that are coming your way. A prospective franchise owner needs to understand this.

That is why it is so important to have an accountant and lawyer by your side as you go through the process. They can provide you with the information and guidance to help you make the best decisions for you and your new business. Do NOT place your faith and future into the franchise owners! They have their interests as their first priority and you need someone with YOUR interests as their top priority.

But their advice will only do you good if you hear it and follow it. Do NOT think you know better and do not allow your clouded judgment to overall them because you so desperately want to follow your dream and own your own business. Sometimes your dreams do not have to be abandoned, they just need to be postponed just a little bit.

After all, if waiting a few months or another year will give you a much better chance of building a successful business, isn't it worthwhile to pay attention to the advice and wait?

What are the Limitations of Owning the Franchise?

When is your business really not your business? When you own a franchise. After all, when you own a franchise you agree to follow their business model and adhere to their rules and policies. You cannot market or run your business any way you see fit. It must follow the franchise model.

Because of this, there will be restrictions on what you can and can't do when it comes to operating your business. From things like changing the franchise log (a huge no-no!) to setting your own prices or carrying other products, you will need to check to see what is and is not allowed.

Here are just a few of the possible limitations you might find yourself subjected to as a franchise owner:

Business Model

Franchises usually require you to follow their business model to the letter of its description. That means you have to do everything the way they say it should be done. If changes are necessary, or if changes will enhance the ability of the franchise to be successful, those changes must be submitted and approved by the parent company before they can be instituted.

This means that you are not free to run your business as you see fit even though it is your business. You have to run your franchise the same way as all the other franchisees do so that if a customer walks in to your franchise or to anyone else's, they will get the same treatment, the same products and have the same "feel" for the business regardless of the location or owner.

Appearance and Design

For better or worse, brand recognition also depends a lot on appearance and design. If you take the time to notice, you will find that most franchises look the same on the exterior and interior. The layout will be similar if not exact, the logo will be the same and the signage and other parts of the business will be the same as well.

Most franchises have established building plans and even approved contractors who are familiar with the building style and requirements as indicated by the parent company.

The franchise owner might have some discretion or leeway but usually other than choosing which set of plan from the parent company, the franchisee has little leeway when it comes to what their building or layout looks like.

The reason for this is the same as for using the same business model. The focus is on the customer having the same experience regardless of which location they go into or who owns that location. If the customer does not feel at home because the franchise looks or feels different, that damages the overall brand value.

Customer Service Policies

Whether you are opening a franchise location or your own business, how you treat your customers will often be the deciding factor as to whether or not your business will succeed. If you treat your customer's right, and they feel they received a good value from you and your business, they will come back again and again. If they are treated poorly, they will leave and never come back. So you need to do it right the first time because you might never get a second chance.

Customer Service, and the policies that surround it, are also important parts of the brand image.

Not only do we want every customer to get the same feel and impression, we also want them to get the same products and the same level of service that they equate with that particular brand.

Site Approval

Some franchisees must have their site pre-approved by the parent company to help insure that it is a good fit and has a likely chance for success. They will evaluate the location and surrounding market and either approve or turn down the site request.

This helps the franchisee get the best possible site even though it might not be in the location initially desired or requested. But the franchise parent company has a track record and knowledge of what the ideal markets are and can often times better evaluate sites than the potential owner even though he may be from that particular area.

Sales Area

Some franchises limit the physical area in which you can market your business and sell your products. They do this to protect existing and future franchisees that might purchase a location in another area. After all, you do not want to pay your franchisee fee and then all of a sudden find the same franchise opening up a new location the next block over!

This might also come into play if you intend to market your product or services on-line as well. Many businesses make a large percentage of their sales online at the expense of those who own physical stores. Internet companies can sell at lower prices because they do not have the expenses associated with a brick and mortar store. To level the playing field a bit, some franchises are prohibited from selling anything outside their physical location.

You might also be prohibited from selling outside of your geographical area as well. For example you might be licensed to sell within your state but not out of state. This is done to protect the locations in that state from losing their sales to an online vendor or outside the area vendor with lower prices.

Product Selection

Some franchises limit the products that can be sold to the products they produce and make available to their franchisees. A perfect example of this would be the national burger franchises that all sell the same menu items. If you buy a burger at a franchise location you get one delivered to the location from the parent company or by an approved supplier. You do NOT get a locally made burger from a supermarket or warehouse store.

While that is commonplace, other franchises might limit you to having to purchase all your products through them even if identical materials and products can be purchased elsewhere for less.

Another thing to look into is whether or not you would be allowed to add items to your product offering if they are regional or local favorites. Some franchises will allow you to do so while many others will not. It is good to have this discussion up front so that you know before you sign whether you can add other products or not.

Materials & Supplies

One way some franchises increase their profits is by requiring individual franchises to purchase EVERYTHING through the parent company. That means not only products but supplies such as napkins, cleaning products, toilet tissue and everything else. The parent company places a surcharge onto their cost and then makes a profit on every purchase.

This is important to know upfront because you could very well be "held hostage" by the parent company because you committed to buy from them and only them. So they are free to charge whatever they want to charge and you would be forced to pay it. This might be another cost of doing business that you might not have with another similar franchise.

Pricing

Though there are laws against price fixing, it is common to pay pretty much the same price for the same product within a geographical area. Metropolitan areas might charge more because their expenses are greater. But the parent company would prefer that all locations keep their prices the same so the customer is not happier with one location over another.

This is also important to the other franchisees in an area. If you charge $2.00 for a burger and 10 other location in your area charge the same $2.00, people will be conditioned or expected to pay $2.00 for that burger. But if one new owner decides to charge $1.50 for the same burger, he is going to steal sales from other dealers and cause customers to feel negatively about the other dealers.

This is a common strategy when one business wants to capture a larger share of the market or drive another business out of business. They reduce prices until the other business cannot afford to match the lower price and they go out of business. Because of this franchises take great measures to insure the security of all their franchises against this sort of activity.

In this particular case, price restrictions can help protect your business against the actions of other franchisees.

Renewal of Lease or Agreement

Some franchise agreements are for life and some are for a limited time frame such as 20 or 25 years. When the end of the agreement is reached then new terms are negotiated between the franchise owner and the parent company. If the agreement is permanent then you own the rights to operate the franchise subject to the conditions of the contract.

Your lawyer is critical at this point. Make sure the wording of the contract clearly spells out your exact rights both for now and in the future. The last thing you want is to spend your time and money building a business only to lose it later when the franchise refuses to extend the agreement.

Ability to Sell Franchise

Sometimes we reach a point where we want to sell our business. Either it has become profitable and we want to sell it while it is worth more or whether we determined that this is not the business for us. Either way, we want to sell it and either recoup our investment or turn a profit.

You want to make sure there are no restrictions on your ability to sell your franchise to another person when you feel the time is right. Some franchises might want or demand you sell it back to them only.

This not only limits your options but also usually means you will not get the full value from the sale like you might with a competitive selling environment.

Restrictions will always be part of any franchise agreement. They really have to be to ensure a uniform experience for the customer regardless of where they might go. That is part of the confidence in going to a franchise location. If you like the experience in your home town, chances are you will also like it across the state or across the country.

Understand that certain restrictions are in place to help the parent company retain their brand image. But there are others that are in place to protect the franchisee as well. Anything that helps protect the brand and ensures the best overall customer experience actually benefits both the franchisee and the parent company.

Franchisees must understand that what the other franchisees do will affect their business and vice versa. If someone gets a bad burger or a stale bagel in California, they might drive by your location selling the same brand in Florida because they equate the bad experience not just with the individual location but with the brand itself.

People go where they have the best experiences and get the best treatment and the best value. If either of those is missing because someone didn't follow the rules or play fair, the entire brand can suffer.

At the same time, sometimes the parent company will hide behind the uniform experience excuse for instituting all kind of restrictions designed to increase profits for the parent company at the expense of the individual franchisees. Personally, if I go into a burger franchise and get a great tasting burger, I'm happy. It makes little difference to me whether the toilet paper came from a local store or the parent company.

But hey, that's just me.

What Are the Success and Failure Rates?

We have already mentioned the fact that just purchasing a franchise does not mean you will soon be printing money hand over fist and living in a gated community with free dock space for your 110 foot yacht. Just because you buy a franchise does not guarantee you that it will be profitable. There are risks in every kind of business and franchising is no different.

Good franchises carefully choose their owners and locations to give everyone the best chances for success. They will monitor the market and compare one market against a similar established one to get a pretty good idea whether that is an area that will do well. That is what good franchise will do. Unfortunately, not all franchises are created equal.

Some franchises will sell as many locations in any area as long as someone has the franchise fee and is willing to spend it on one of their franchises.

These franchises are in it for the money first and the brand second and that is not a good thing for the company and all their franchise owners.

But no matter how much preparation and study and analysis that the new owner or parent company might do, nothing is guaranteed and no one really knows until the building is built and the business opens. Only then will we see how customers will respond to that new location. That means some locations will prosper, others will struggle and a few will close their doors within the first year or two.

That is why it is important to ask the parent company for their statistics on success and failures of new locations for the first 5 years. If they say they have no failures, then you might consider packing up your briefcase and trying somewhere else because they probably are not being truthful with you. Even the best franchise has locations that fail.

There are many reasons for a location failing. It could be the area and people who live there. It might be the owner of that location that was the cause of the problems. It could be the parent company. There might be too much competition. Whatever the reasons might be, it is important that you know those reasons and see if any apply to you and your location.

You might want to consider involving your accountant at this point to take a look at those locations that failed and understand why that happened. Perhaps the new owners were under financed or just poor businessmen. Your accountant should be able to tell a lot from the financial history of failed franchises. I should mention that the parent company might not be willing to share specific information because this was not their business. In fact, privacy rules and regulations might prohibit the sharing of this information.

If there are poorly performing locations that are still in business but just hanging on by a thread you might want to talk to the owners or managers of one or two of those locations. You can learn a lot by talking to people in these types of locations. It is a lot easier for someone to brag about their over performing store than it is for someone to talk openly about the problems they are having with their business. In those cases, sometimes ego's get in the way of being open and honest.

This is just one more area where knowing these things up front can help you make the very best and most accurate decisions on whether this franchise and this location is the right thing for you. It is much cheaper and easier to change your mind now before the building is built and the contracts are signed.

Sometimes the franchise is good and sound but the location is just a poor match between the products and services and the people in that area. If that is the case then things might be resolved by simply changing your location to an area much better suited to that franchises products and services.

You do not have to give up your dreams; you just need to be aware of how to best turn those dreams into your own personal reality. You do that by getting as much factual and relevant information as you possibly can. That means both positive and negative information. Sometimes you can learn a lot more from negative information because it highlights weaknesses and failures of that particular business model.

Does the Whole Thing Make Sense to You?

There comes a time when you have all the information you can possibly and have researched to the best of your ability. You have listened to other people like your accountant, your lawyer, even your family members and friends and have all their advice and recommendations. But the honest truth is that this is your decision and only you can really make it.

Some people love the franchise business model because it spells out everything you need to do and exactly how you need to do it. All of this knowledge comes from people like you trying to create the best and most profitable business. All their trial and error helps you get results faster and more easily.

But all of this comes at a price and sometimes that price can be pretty steep. The franchise fee itself is often enough to discourage many people from taking that first step and making the commitment. After all, if you don't have the money, you don't have the money. Some people cannot get financing or credit either and in those cases, sometimes the decision is made for you already.

The one question you should be asking yourself before you make your decision is really a simple question with a whole lot of answers. The question is "Does it make sense to you?" If it doesn't make sense to you for whatever reason that means you have discovered a weakness or shortcoming in the franchise. Or maybe it just means that the franchise way of going into business is just not right for you.

Maybe you don't like following orders or instructions. Maybe you like to do things your way. Neither of those makes you a bad person or even a bad businessman. But they might make you a very poor franchise candidate. Franchise people need to be able to follow orders and follow procedures, especially in the beginning. The brand requires it from everyone and you cannot be the exception.

While I cannot advise you on whether a particular franchise would be right for you, I would offer you the following advice when it comes to making your final decision.

Here are the things I would consider if I were you. This is not a 100% all inclusive list and you might have a few other things to add. But this list will give you a pretty good indication of whether franchising is right for you or not?

Are Your Comfortable With the Entire Business Model?

Everyone has a case of the nerves whenever they commit to anything new or go out of their comfort zone. Nervousness is normal and is one of the ways we keep from doing things that place us in danger like skydiving and bungee jumping. But we cannot allow a simple case of the nerves to keep us from moving forward in life.

But if you have some very real and strong reservations or concerns about any part of the process, then you should postpone your decision or abandon it is the concerns are serious enough. Do more research, talk to more people, ask more questions and do whatever you can to either relieve your concerns or help you look for something else.

Intuition and feelings often will keep us from making terrible mistakes. So listen to that little voice in the back of your head and follow your intuition.

Can You Afford it?

If you don't have the money to not only pay the fees and start your business but also fund it through the period of time when you are not making a lot of sales then you should either hold off until you do have the money or look for a less expensive alternative.

Talk to your accountant and get their recommendations as well. Beware of taking out a lot of loans and financing. If your business should fail you will be left with a ton of debt and nothing to show for it.

Never commit your life savings or other money that you cannot afford to lose into a new business. For example, if you are 60, do not cash in your entire retirement savings and use it to start your own business. If it should fail you would be left with no retirement savings and almost no time to start over.

In other words, just be financially responsible and listen to your accountant. After all, that is what you are paying them for, isn't it?

What Does Your Accountant and Lawyer Think About it?

Let's just keep this one short and sweet. Run everything past your lawyer and accountant. Then listen to what they tell you and advise you. If you don't agree then get a second opinion. But don't think you know better than they do because you almost certainly don't.

You might get lucky but the odds are severely stacked against you if you ignore the advice of your professionals.

How Does Your Family Feel About it?

If you are single then the decisions you make involve just you. But if you are married or engaged or have other people in your life that care about you or depend on you, then any decisions you make will affect them as well. Therefore it would make sense to seek their feelings on your new business plans. If they are supportive then that's great. But if they are against it or have serious concerns about it, you owe them the right to voice their opinions and concerns to you.

Keep in mind that at the very beginning of your business you will be putting in more time and effort into your business and that means less time home with friends and family. Everyone needs to be aware of this in the beginning and agree to this. If this is not possible for a number of reasons this should factor into your decision in a very serious manner.

After all, if it costs you your family and friends in order to start your business is it really worth it? Most people would say no but this is your life and your decision. But always factor in family and friends into your decision.

Do You Feel that You Did the Proper Amount of Research?

Any time you are risking your life savings, you need to be as sure as possible in what you are doing. Having a dream is one thing but if you cannot turn that dream into a reality then perhaps it is best left as a dream.

Look into everything as thoroughly as possible. Ask any question that pops into your head. If you don't understand something learn about it before moving forward. Don't believe everything people tell you no matter how much you want to believe it. Spend the time to confirm everything you are told.

Dispute things that don't make sense to you. Make people prove things to you. Make them show you proof like financial statements and other irrefutable proof. If they don't want to show it to you there is a reason for that. If people are being evasive, walk away until you can be sure.

Don't believe outrageous claims of easy money and huge profits. As your mother and father probably told you, if it sounds too good to be true it probably is. Do your homework and don't stop until you honestly feel you have done as much as you possibly can. Then get the accountant and lawyer involved and get their views because committing to anything.

Have You Been Honest and Up-Front With Yourself Throughout the Entire Process?

Sometimes we want something so bad we do everything in our power to convince ourselves that this is the right thing for us to do. That includes convincing ourselves we have skills we really don't have, that we are willing to work harder and longer than we know we can. We tell ourselves that we are someone we are not because this is what we have to be to make this whole thing work.

When a question comes up about you and your skills or abilities, answer it as painfully honest as you possibly can. Do not lie to yourself or dismiss something because it might stand in your way. You know who and what you are and that should be as close a match to the franchise as possible.

If you are not truthful about everything you might wind up biting off more than you can chew or be totally miserable all the time in your business. That is something no one wants. If you cannot be happy doing what you need to do then you should look for something else. No one can create a successful business is they are unhappy all the time.

YA Gotta Believe!

More than anything, you have to honestly believe that the whole thing is right for you and that you have what it takes to create the business and bring it to success.

If you are unsure on any part of the process or the franchise itself, it is time to stop and rethink things.

You should be excited about the opportunity and really believe that this is going to be the best decision you have ever made. You should not be unsure or doubtful. You can be nervous because this is a huge step in your life but you should believe in yourself and your abilities.

This might seem like a little thing but if you really believe in something you will give it your best effort. When we have doubts or we are unsure about something we often look for excuses to back off or give up. There is no room for that kind of attitude when it comes to building a new business.

Getting the
Right Training

When it comes to doing anything new or different, knowledge is power. After all, if you don't something the right way, you are bound to get less than stellar results! That is why training, support and knowledge are so important when it comes to starting out on the right foot in your franchise business.

Most of the time your franchise will offer you training to help you get started. My advice to you is to take whatever classes they offer and learn everything you possibly can from those who have already done it. Even if the training does not exactly pertain to you or your situation, take it anyway. Anything you can do to learn more about the business and more about the operation will help you in the long run. Here is one important rule that I have always lived by that has never once let me down:

If the training is free, take it. If you have the opportunity to learn something, learn it.

To the best of my knowledge no one has ever complained that they knew too much about something. When it comes to you and your business, the more you know the better decisions you will make. The more you know the faster you will be able to do things and do them with better results.

Here are some of the best ways to get the knowledge and skills you will need to create and run a successful business:

Company Provided Training

If you purchase a franchise, you are also purchasing their specific business model. You will need training on how to follow their model and operate your location in the same manner that others operate theirs. This is important for brand recognition and continuity of the customer experience.

To achieve this most franchises will offer some kind of training to make sure everyone learns the right way to do things. This training might be in the form of a manual, classroom sessions, videos, or other forms of learning.

Sometimes you might have the option of choosing which form of training you would like to take.

videos are great, in-person training where you can ask questions and learn from others is usually the way to go. This way you can share experiences and listen to the questions of others. Usually if someone has a question others are wondering the same thing. So everyone benefits.

Again, if you have the ability to take any kind of training from the parent company and it is included in your franchise license, take it. You never know when that knowledge will come in handy even though you might not need it today.

On the Job Training

Sometimes certain things do not translate well into videos or books or manuals. Sometimes you really need to watch someone do it and then do it yourself. This is where you learn the real world practical information pertaining to your business.

Some franchises will require you to work in one of their other locations prior to opening your own. This is for both your benefit and the franchises benefit. Understanding what needs to be done on a daily basis and actually doing it can help you hit the ground running when your doors open.

Don't look at on the job training as a waste of your time

You will almost always pick up a few things that weren't covered in the book or training manual. The end result is that you will be able to do more things and do them in less time when you learn by actually doing it.

College or Technical School

Some colleges offer a ton of business related courses from accounting to customer service to inventory control. There are many individual skills required to correctly run a small business. Very few of us have all of them when we start. But a few college level courses can give you the high level skills you will need to understand things from day one.

Training on Your Own

Books, tapes, educational television, seminars, videos and other forms of learning make it possible for anyone to learn almost everything these days. After all, you are learning the ins and outs of franchising from this book, right?

If you think you need to learn something, you probably do. If you have difficulty doing something, you probably could use some better or more current skills. If something seems way above your skill set, that is an indication of the need for some advanced training as well.

Skills also do not stay current forever, either. So what once were good skills might now be hopelessly outdated. There will be new knowledge, new technology and other things that you need to keep up to date on. That is why everyone should make it a priority not only to learn new things, but to update that knowledge every year as well. It is much easier to update skills each year than to try and "catch up" on 20 years of missing information at one time!

Don't Wait Until You Need the Skills!

One problem a lot of people have is that they don't bother learning something until they need it in real life. The problem with that approach is that it takes time to learn things and during that time you might make poor decisions or miss out on important opportunities.

Training is much easier when it is done on a pro-active basis. That means discovering which skills and knowledge you need and then getting that knowledge before you need it. This allows you to do your learning on your own schedule without the pressure and tight deadlines that usually accompany learning that is done on an emergency basis.

Set up a training program with dates next to each skill that you want to learn each topic by.

This will help keep you on track and motivated. Learning can be fun if you approach it in the right way. Think of training as a way to make your business more successful and easier to run. Do not think of training as a chore or a job. Think of it as improving yourself to help you become a better and more efficient person.

Get Business Training

There are several reasons why people decide to open their own business. Some people do it so they do not have to work for someone else or make someone else rich from their labors. Others may do it because they see the wealthy people who got wealthy from their own business. Some people see their skills as a good fit to make a lot more money than they currently earn. Last, some people think that owning their own business is an easier way to earn a living.

It doesn't make much difference which group you are in. You are going to start your own business because you want to and the reasons behind that decision are up to you. But unless you have owned your own business before, you are definitely going to need to get some new skills and have someone show you the basics involved in running your own business.

I have always believed that the best training for running your own business is to run someone else's business. This way someone else will be on the hook for your mistakes and not you. Because you will make mistakes until you become comfortable not only with what you learned from your research and from books, but also from what you learned from real-life experience.

Business training does not refer to learning procedures and rules and how to mix coffee or cook a burger. Instead, business training involves all the skills you need to operate your business, hire employees, make sure your inventory is properly managed and reduce or eliminate waste and other problems that could wind up costing you a ton of money is you don't stay on top of things.

You should know how to read financial statements and reports as well as profit and loss statements. You should be able to manage your inventory so that you always have the products you need when you need them but not by carrying too much inventory at the same time. Everyone can solve their inventory problems by buying more than they will ever need. But that costs money and expenses come out of the profits.

Now some people might say that this is precisely why you have an accountant and lawyer at your disposal and they would be 100% correct in making that statement.

But since this is YOUR business and because it will be YOUR signature on the paperwork and because YOU will be ultimately responsible for everything pertaining to your business, YOU need to know what you are doing and what is going on with your business.

Many a business has failed because the owners did not keep a close eye on the financials of their business. Many a business has been gutted by people who took advantage of a clueless owner that blindly trusted people to do the right thing. But the reality was that people were stealing money from the owner's pockets and the owner had no idea what was going on as it was happening.

Another area where you will need to get some training is the rules, regulations and requirements for businesses in your town and state. If you miss a tax payment, you will pay a penalty. If you fail to adhere to a requirement because you didn't know it existed, you will pay a penalty or fine. Ignorance of the law is no excuse. As a business owner, franchise or otherwise, you are expected to know what you need to do and you are responsible for doing it.

The time for getting this training is before you open the doors on your new business. Ideally it should be before you decide on which franchise you want to get in with.

You should get some business training and some real life experience working in your own business, or a friends business, so you can be aware of what is involved especially in the beginning.

At this stage of the game, where you have made your decision but not made a commitment yet, getting more business training will help you negotiate things better and also give you an extremely accurate accounting of what it would be like to own a similar business.

Business training will also make you aware of things you will need to do or follow when it comes to running your business. These can be minor things that can be easily accomplished or they can be very expensive and labor intensive requirements that you might not be willing to accept. As with so many other things, it is best to discover this now rather than later.

Invest a little bit of time and money now so you can learn what you need to know before you need to actually know it. Then you can help keep your business on the right tack because you will understand everything that is involved in operating your kind of business in your town. As we said, it is much better to develop these skills now rather than later when it might be too late.

Getting the Right Support

No matter how skilled we are and no matter how hard we are willing to work, there will always be someone who can do things faster and better than we can. After all, no matter who you are you cannot be the best at everything. This doesn't mean you don't have the aptitude to become the best, it just means that you aren't quite there yet.

So we can all agree that we are likely to need some help starting our business. We need someone to show us the way to go and how to do the things we need done to make out business a success. The good news is that franchises usually have a support feature built into their business plan.

A support program means that there are resources available to the business owners to help answer questions, resolve problems, make decisions and generally assist with all business related activities. This kind of help can be critical for the new franchisee.

Chances are that whatever you come up against, the support team has been there, done that and can guide you in the right direction.

Support usually takes two forms. There might be a number to call to access the support desk or you might have a franchise supervisor assigned to your particular location. This rep will visit your store, talk to you about your business and discuss financial issues and results with you to let you know how you are doing. The rep will probably also be accessible by phone for emergency issues.

When evaluating a franchise opportunity, the type of support they provide should be an important consideration. If they provide on-going support for as long as you remain a franchise owner, that is very good. If they only provide it for a short time after your business is running, that should be a concern. After all, your continued success is not only in your best interest but in the franchises best interest as well. Higher sales mean more fee and more fees mean higher income for the franchise.

Ask specific questions about what kind of support will be available to you after you sign up. Ask if you will have a supervisor or other support professional assigned to you or if you would be sharing a group of supervisors.

Personally, I like the dedicated supervisor or support professional because you can develop a relationship with you and your location. This will enable them to spot trends and discover problems, or successes, faster.

Sometimes franchise owners will hire their own support to help them get started as a new business owner. You might hire someone who has previous experience in your particular franchise who will come in and get things running quickly as you watch and learn. There is a cost associated with this kind of support but it can help immeasurably in the beginning.

There are also business consultants that are available to show you how to do just about anything when it comes to your business. If you are weak or unsure about anything, you might want to sit down and talk to a consultant to see how you can learn about that topic and how they can help you get the skills you need.

Another important thing to understand is that if support is made available to you, use it. It is part of your package and the cost for it has already been built into the franchise fee structure. So you would be foolish if you didn't take full advantage of it.

If you do take advantage of the support, pay attention and listen to what you are being told.

Don't think you know more than the support professional because there is a pretty darned good chance that you don't. They have the knowledge and real world experience that you probably lack in the beginning so ask, listen and learn from your support people.

Most support people are accustomed to a lot of questions and calls from new franchisees. Do not feel that you are burdening them by asking too many questions. That is their job and they will usually answer every question and help you as best they can. What usually happens is that there are a lot of questions in the beginning and the questions and calls gradually decline over time as the new franchisee learns more and becomes more confident. This is totally normal.

Keep in mind, though, that support and supervisory personnel are there to HELP you do your job and not to do it for you. They will give you advice and information but it is up to you to implement your new found knowledge. In other words, ask them for help not to do something for you so you can do something else. The only way you will learn is by paying attention and doing what they tell you to do.

When talking to other franchise owners during your research, ask them about how much support they get from the parent company

The answer to that question could speak volumes about how the franchise feels about their owners. If they give support a priority, it indicates they truly want their owners to be successful. If they offer little to no support, then that should make you question if they are interested in you or just the fees you pay. It is something to think about.

One last thing about support and your business. Do not for one minute feel that you are weak or less intelligent because you are asking people for help and support. The reality of it is that asking for help, and admitting you need help, indicate a lot of strength and confidence and not weakness. If you need help it is much better to get it than be afraid to ask for it. Not getting the help you need may result in taking longer to get your business up and running and might even lead to going out of business

So if help and support is available to you, use it. If your franchise offers a lot of support, that's a great thing. But even the most all encompassing support is worth nothing if you don't use it and follow it. Don't let pride or ego stand in the way of asking for or getting help. Everyone needs help and support at sometime in their lives.

So use it.

Part Three:

The Path to Success!

Improving Your Communication Skills

This is one of those areas that everyone thinks they do just fine with. But the facts are that most of us are pretty poor communicators. We make simple mistakes that keep us from being as successful or efficient as we can be. The result is confusion, mistakes and wasted resources.

When it comes to running your own business, the ability to communicate actively and effectively can mean the difference between success and failure or profit and loss. So we need to understand just what is involved in proper communication so we can learn how to improve and allow our new business to run smoother and better.

Two Way Process

First and foremost, communication is a two way process. It consists of both listening and speaking.

If you do not do both you are not communicating effectively. You need to both know what you are saying and understand what is being said by the other person or people.

Even though you are an owner, communication about your business is not like a dictatorship. It is not just what you say that is important. Employees and other people involved in your business have important things to share and tell you as well. You need to have an open mind and listen to what others are telling you or you will miss out on some potentially important information or insight.

You Cannot Multi-Task in Communication

Contrary to what you might think, you just cannot talk and listen at the same time and do both effectively. Whenever the brain tries to do more than one thing at a time it divides resources accordingly. So if you are trying to talk and listen at the same time or do your e-mails or financial reports while talking with someone, both activities are likely to suffer.

When someone else is talking, listen to what they have to say and take it all in. Do not talk over them or interrupt them. Not only is this rude and disrespectful, it interferes with the efficient free flowing of information between those involved in the conversation.

Let the other people stop talking, wait a few seconds and then respond.

You should also stop trying to formulate your response while others are still talking. Not only will you miss information but you might be concentrating so hard on what your response is going to be that you misunderstand what the other person is saying in the first place.

The bottom line is if you are engaged in a conversation; give it your full attention. Make sure only one of you is talking at the same time and think about your response only when the other person has finished their thought. Doing one thing at a time will help you get more accurate information and allow the entire communication process to go more smoothly and efficiently.

Do Not Communicate When People are Angry

Always try to communicate with other people when everyone is calm. When people are upset or angry they sometimes put up a kind of wall where they refuse to really listen to what you are saying. It is like they have already made up their mind about what you are going to say and they don't like it one bit!

Emotions make it difficult and sometimes impossible to accurately communicate with others.

Things get taken out of context, other things get exaggerated, and the overall details of the communication become distorted and inaccurate.

Instead of trying to force communication with angry people, try and calm things down first and bring the tension in the room to as near as normal as possible. Reassure the person that you are trying to help them and get them to calm down. Only when you feel they are calm enough should you try to get into an actual conversation with them. Sometimes it is best to put off the conversation a bit until cooler heads will prevail.

Hear More than Just the Words

One common problem occurs when the person who is listening only hears the words and not the emotions or voice behind them. Only about 10% of what we say is contained in the words we use. The other 90% comes from the tone of our voice, our mannerisms and body language, and our facial expressions. All of those things contain our emotions and other information that can communicate the seriousness or importance of the topic much more clearly.

Make it a habit to observe the other people as they are speaking and listening to try and get a glimpse of their emotional state.

Very often when we know how a person is really feeling we will change the words we use to deliver the message in a certain way designed to make the person feel better and more relaxed. The only way we can successfully do this is by understanding the other person emotional state before hand.

Be Specific and Very Clear in Your Communication

When you own a business, certain things have to be done a certain and specific way in order for everything to turn out the same way every time and every day. To make sure this happens, you not only must be able to communicate what needs to be done but exactly how you want it done.

This is especially important when you are dealing with something very new or when you are teaching a new employee or an older employee that you are teaching so that they can have increased responsibility. The more accurate and specific your communication and instructions are, the less chance you will have that something will be done in the wrong manner.

For example, you could tell an employee to "Close the store promptly at 9PM and close out the registers before you leave." That tells the employee what needs to be done but gives them very little detail.

It increases the chances that something might be missed or done incorrectly or in such a way that the result would not be valid.

A much better instruction might be: "Close the store at 9PM and close out the register after you lock the doors. Count the money in the cash drawer and run the daily summary reports by selecting reports from the drop down menu. Then put the cash and the reports in the safe and make sure it is locked. Then clear the register so everything will be set to zero for the next day. Make sure to empty the garbage and set the alarm before you leave.

As you can easily see, this gives more specific information about what needs to be done and when it needs to be done. There are several tasks listed so the employee will have a clear understanding of what has to happen before they leave at the end of the day.

Business communication needs to be specific so you can be reasonably sure that procedures and policies will be followed as closely as possible. Remember, when you own a franchise there are specific things that need to be done at certain times and everyone needs to be aware of those things. As the owner this is your responsibility to make sure everyone understands exactly what needs to be done.

Summarize the Outcome of the Conversation

In business, many conversations revolve around something that needs to be done or needs to happen. You might have an hour meeting or conversation about who is supposed to do what and when it is supposed to be done. Sometimes these conversations involve more than one person.

Because of this it is a great idea to have a short recap of what was just talked about and everyone's assignments or responsibilities gone over one last time so everyone is crystal clear on what is supposed to happen next. This allows everyone a last opportunity to ask for clarification and ask questions as well.

Good communications are very important in all aspects of our lives but especially so in our businesses. This was just a short highlight of some of the basics of communications. It is not intended as a complete resource. I would suggest that everyone reading this book also pick up a book on communication skills and brush up on their own skills. Even though everyone thinks they communicate just fine right now, almost everyone will benefit by going over how to communicate effectively. Even if you just pick up one or two small things from the training that might make your business run much smoother with fewer mistakes and far less confusion.

Develop a Business Plan & Then Work that Plan!

One of the best parts about purchasing a franchise is that they already have designed a business plan for you to follow. But while that plan will help guide you in turning your new business into a success, it is not going to do everything you need to help you in your particular situation.

What you are going to need is a plan that takes the ideas and goals that are in your head and turns them into a plan that you can follow. A plan that will give you specific information on how well you are doing and whether or not you are on pace to make your dreams come true.

For example, let's say you went through your research and decided on a franchise location and have already discussed everything with your accountant.

You have looked at the financial data and projected sales for the next year or two and you have agreed that this all makes sense and you have some specific expectations for your new business.

Your plan will take those expectations and put them on paper and the result is going to be a plan with some very real and specific goals that you should be able to meet if your research and analysis was correct. But no research or analysis is always 100% correct in predicting the future. If it was, everyone would be millionaires and no business would ever fail.

For example, let's say you and your accountant figured during your research that your first months sales should be $10,000 and those sales should increase by 5% every month for the first two years as you become more widely known within the area. Those were the figures and estimates you used to determine if this business could be successful. Based on those figures you determined that it could be. So it makes sense that those figures should be your initial goals.

So your business plan would list the first month's sales at $10,000 and the next month's sales at $10,500 (5% increases each month) and then do the same month after month. You then have a stated goal for where you thought your business could perform.

You then can compare your sales against these figures and know at a glance how you are doing.

If you sell $15,000 the first month that is great! You are ahead of goal and things look good for you and your business. But if you sold $2,000 that first month, you would know that should be somewhat of a concern because you projected much higher. Now sales can be higher one month and lower the next month but the important thing is that you have a plan to consult that will give you a baseline for where you need to be.

If you are like most business owners you will also have a plan for growing your business or establishing yourself in the community. So those two areas would also be in your business plan as well. You would identify events or marketing programs designed to increase awareness of your business. You would track your advertising and promotions budget so you would know what you should or shouldn't do.

The whole point of having your own business plan is to give you an easy way of tracking budgets and performance so that YOU can monitor things from YOUR point of view to protect YOUR best interests! You and your accountant can devise a plan that helps you grow your business responsively according to your available money and resources. You plan can be changed when sales increase over your estimates and it can be revised if they fall below estimates.

A business plan from your franchise company will give you expectations but these are not always designed with your best interests at heart. They might want more money spent on advertising even if that isn't smart because more advertising gets the brand more exposure without it costing the parent company a dime! While most franchises will work closely with you to help insure your future success, you should never allow a parent company to make decisions for you and your business.

The biggest benefit to having a business plan is that a good and accurate business plan allows you to respond faster and more accurately to changes within your business. Without a way to measure things, something might go on for months until you become aware of it. During those months you could be losing money or market share to your competition. But if you had a good business plan with clear and easily recognizable goals, you would be able to see potential problems a lot easier and faster.

The most successful business owners are the ones that know the most about their business and are able to react faster and more accurately when things change. This might mean adjusting inventory because sales are far higher than you thought and you could risk losing sales because you didn't have enough stock. Or, on the negative side, you might stay with a non performing product for too long because you weren't aware of lowering sales.

In the worst case, you would not discover that your business was not profitable until you had spent money for several months trying to wait for profits that would likely never come.

Many business owners will have more than one plan. They might have a 1 year plan, a 5 year plan and a 10 year plan. All of these plans will include hopes and dreams of where they want their business to be at the end of a certain period of time. If something changes to make those plans not possible or much harder to achieve, then we can go back into our plans and change them to reflect our new reality. That does not mean we failed, it just means that things have changed and that our plans did their job and made us aware of that. So we change our plans to make them achievable again and move on.

Consider you business plan as a tool in your business tool box. Consider it something that will guide you towards more accurate decisions in less time. Consider it a resource that will make it easier and less stressful to operate and grow your business. Business plans allow you to be pro-active instead of reactive and that is almost always the best way to go not just in business but in life as well.

Last, but most certainly not least, your business plan will help you become more motivated and then stay motivated.

Life becomes more exciting when we actually see our progress as it happens. When we work hard for a month and see our sales grow because of that hard work, it gives us incentive and encouragement to keep up the hard work. If you do something and are not aware of the results, you might stop doing it even though it really was working great. You just didn't see it because you didn't know how to measure it.

Go get with your accountant and other support people and devise your new business plan. Give it specific goals with specific deadlines. Make those goals achievable and realistic. If you have to go back and readjust something, go ahead. But stick with your plan and your plan will help you grow.

Taking a Hands-On Approach

Though this applies to any kind of business, we will be concentrating on franchises when it comes to having a hands-on approach to your business.

Even though this is a franchise and a lot of the planning and problem solving has been done for you, operating a franchise is not a hands-off process. The owner is going to have to be involved even if they hire a manager to run things for them. This is important to understand because no one can own a business and then totally distance themselves from it.

Your business is your business and the responsibility for running it properly does not lie with any one employee or even all the employees. The final responsibility lies with the owner. Think about that for a moment. If your business is run poorly, who suffers? Well, you do because sales will be lower and expenses will likely be higher.

While a few employees might suffer because they will lose their jobs or have their hours cut back, the one who will suffer the most is you, the owner.

If you hire a manager and one day the manager leaves for a better job, your business still has to go on and someone is going to have to know how to operate things when needed. Managers also get sick and take vacations and have personal issues as well. Unfortunately, managers are not immune to passing away suddenly like many people do each year either.

Though I do not mean to be morbid, the point I am trying to make is that the owner must have a hands-on approach to managing and running their business. While they can hire people to perform vital functions, they still need to know what is involved in performing those functions and why they need to be done in the first place. This ensures that the success of the business will not be tied to just one or two critical employees.

I have always thought that the new owner of the business should have to work at every position within the business. They should man the counter, handle inventory, unload trucks, ride along on deliveries and any other task that is present in the company.

They need to do this not to prove they can do everything but so they KNOW everything that goes on in their business. They will get to experience problems and shortfalls in the system by actually working within that system. When it comes to hiring they will be able to understand what the position entails and what kind of person is best suited for that position. After all, a different kind of person is needed for customer service than is needed for back office work.

This type of knowledge also helps the owner protect themselves against theft and other abuses. If you have worked at a position and know that it takes 15 minutes to do a particular task but one of your employees routinely takes 45 minutes, you will know that there is a problem. If that employee tells you that's how long it should take you will know they are trying to put one over on you.

The same goes for financials and legal issues as well. If you cannot read a financial spreadsheet and rely on others to do that for you, people can cheat you and you might never discover it. Meanwhile you are losing money month after month. There have been story after story about business owners who lost their business or their life savings because they were cheated by their managers or employees.

This does not mean that you have to work 20 hours a day 7 days a week at your business. You can hire employees to handle most of the responsibilities and you can hire managers and supervisors to help monitor things and keep things running smoothly. But you cannot just hire people, walk away and collect profits every month and still expect your business to grow and function at its best.

Employees are far less likely to steal or cheat an involved owner. If you are there watching over things and are an integral part of your business management, people will develop a respect for you and will resist the temptation to take what is not theirs. That means employees will be more careful and honest when an owner spends more time at the business.

Another reason why the owner should develop a hands-on approach is to address changes in the marketplace or industry that can impact sales. You are the owner and are far more likely to understand the market and sales trends than one of your cashiers or supervisors. That mean you will have your eyes and ears focused on your business and will be able to spot trends and issues and capitalize on them much quicker and with greater accuracy.

One of the key aspects of success is surrounding yourself with good people who are highly skilled.

Find as many of these highly skilled people as possible and bring them into your business if the financials indicate that is possible. The more good people you have working in your business the less time you will probably have to work there. But you should never reach the point where some employees don't know who you are and the one's that do haven't seen you in months or even years.

Work at your business, become an informed and knowledgeable owner and you will find yourself more prepared for when something goes wrong and more able to step I when a key employee leaves or is otherwise unavailable. This is not just something every owner should be doing; it is something every owner NEEDS to be doing!

Hiring the Right People

Unless your business defines the term "small business" then you will probably have to hire employees to take care of some of the tasks and responsibilities involved in operating the business and helping customers. It is very rare that one person is able to do everything by themselves and be available every single hour the business is open.

So that means you will have to hire a staff. The first thing to think about is what you can afford as far as payroll is concerned. While you might love to hire 10 employees you might only have the financial resources to hire 5 employees. Unless you cannot possibly avoid it, never hire more people than you can afford or that your business plan indicates you should hire.

Throughout the process, keep one important thing in mind. Your employees will be the face of your business.

Yes, most people will come in the first time or two based on your products and brand recognition, but they will keep coming back time and time again if they feel that their experience was positive and pleasant.

Your employees play a huge role in how that experience will be perceived. They are an extension of you and an extension of your brand. They can either add to the brand or take away from it. They key is hiring the right employees for the right job.

The next thing you should do is carefully consider what your new employees are going to be doing and when they probably will be doing it. Understanding this now will make it easier to hire the right people for each job. After all, you would not want to hire someone, spend time training them, and then realize you need them to work the afternoon shift and then find out they have school or another job then.

Below are a few things to consider when hiring employees. Please note that these are only suggestions and it is not our intent to discriminate against any one person or group of person's. We are also not encouraging anyone to violate any local, state or federal laws when it comes to who you hire either. Our intent is to make you aware of how your employees will affect your business and the customer experience.

With that all said, here are a few things you should consider when hiring employees:

Personality

Personality is a highly subjective quality when it comes to employees. Generally, you want your employees who come in direct contact with your customers to be positive, upbeat, cheerful and helpful. You want your customer to feel positively about your business and who they interact with will have a direct impact on you and your business.

Employees with direct customer contact should honestly want to help the customer. They should enjoy being problem solvers and resolving situations and asking questions. They should also be "people persons" and enjoy interacting with people on a daily basis.

Not everyone enjoys that and not everyone is good at it. Make sure you ask questions pertaining to that in the interviews.

Skill Level

For some positions, specific skills will be required and you should be confident that the applicant either has these skills or has the ability to learn those skills in a relatively short period of time. Since time spent training costs money, look for experience that is as close as possible to what you are looking for.

For example, if you are hiring someone to manage scheduling and payroll, someone who was an office manager in the past would be a good fit. They would just have to adapt to your policies and learn your payroll system. The management part is already in their strengths.

Some people ask which are more important, skills or personality and that is not an easy question to answer. In terms of technical positions of course skill and knowledge are extremely important. After all, a big smile won't be enough to fix your television or diagnose you car's engine properly.

But for position where customer involvement is a major part of your day, personality could very well be more important. After all, you can teach people product knowledge but you can't always teach someone about attitude.

Sometimes it will be a balance but when a position requires specific skills in order to function at a high level, make sure the candidate has those skills or a closely related skill set. It is all about aptitude and the ability to learn.

Education

Education is important for two reasons. First and foremost, specific job related knowledge is critical for someone to function at a high level.

Without the knowledge, someone would have to spend a lot of time learning on the job and that is usually time and money employers either do not have or are willing to spend. So hiring applicants with a higher education in the area which they are being hired for is a plus.

Second, even though their education might not be a direct fit, or even a somewhat close fit, the fact that they have a degree of any kind indicates they have the ability to learn things they are exposed to. So while someone might not have experience in a certain area, the fact that they have a college degree would indicate that they should be able to learn whatever you need them to learn in order to do their job.

There are two other factors that you need to be aware of when it comes to education. The first is cost. People with college degrees, especially advanced degrees, are going to command or at least expect a higher salary. This applies even though the position you are considering them for does not require a degree. So getting someone with a degree and experience might cost you more than you have allocated for the position.

Second, and this can be a tough one at times, when you hire someone with a degree or advanced degree for a lower paying job, you might run the risk of them leaving when a better or higher paying job comes around.

For example, Herb has a Masters Degree in Physics but there are no jobs available now so he goes to work for you at a lower salary so that he can pay his bills and feed his family.

There is nothing wrong with doing that but when you hire someone under those circumstances the time and money you spend training them will be lost when a job I Herb's field, at his accustomed salary, opens up. Then you are back to the beginning having to interview and hire his replacement.

Availability

This is one area where you really should carefully think about what you need and expect from the applicant before you post the job or start interviewing. One of those areas is the time in which you need the person to work.

If you hire someone for the evening shift only to find out you really need them for the morning shift, they might not be able to easily switch shifts. They might have school in the morning or have a child to care for or some other responsibility. You might lose that employee and all the experience and training they had and have to start all over again.

That is not to say that you cannot or should not expect a little flexibility from those that you hire. Having to come in an hour or two early or stay an hour or two later from time to time is not unreasonable. After all, people get sick and go on vacation and when those things happen everyone has to pitch in (including the boss!) and cover for that person.

Where They Live

This is primarily a concern for businesses that operate in areas where weather or traffic is a real concern. These things can hamper or interfere with an employee's ability to get to work on time every day. Their commute will also be longer than usual and this can create a hardship for some people.

Always ask an applicant where they live and how far the commute is. Inquire about how they plan on getting to work as well. Are they driving or taking mass transit? Can they walk to work? Will they be relying on someone else to get them to work and pick them up?

While none of this is your responsibility, when someone doesn't come to work everyone else suffers. So your ideal applicant should have a relatively short and easy commute and not have to rely on other people to get them to and from work.

The bottom line is that closer is better and depending on where your business is located, either driving or mass transit will be better. Understand the area where the potential employee lives and place yourself in their shoes. If it seems like a hardship to you, it probably will seem that way for the employee as well.

The last thing you want is for an applicant to be hired and then realize after a few weeks that the commute is too long and too stressful and then quit. You will then have to hire a replacement and start training all over again.

In some areas, travel is difficult only during certain parts of the day. So you might be able to stagger work shifts and save your employees a lot of time and stress by allowing them to avoid the rush hour travel nightmares. It might be a small gesture on your part that could mean a lot to an employee or two.

Employment History

A major part of running a stable business is maintaining a stable work force. That means low turnover. So when you interview applicants, be aware of people who have gone from job to job to job spending only a few months to a year at each job. That might signal a problem.

If the person constantly improved themselves by the moves, that is one thing. While it still is not good that someone moved so quickly from job to job, it at least provides an explanation. After all, you cannot fault someone for improving themselves and their careers.

But frequent job changes can indicate an inability to work with others, poor work ethic, inferior skills, and other potential problems that required movement to another job. While there might be legitimate reasons for any job move, a pattern of constant movement is usually a reason for concern.

Keep in mind that whenever an employee leaves, the other employees have to work harder until a replacement is found and trained. Plus, the owner or manager has to spend time interviewing and training the new person. Last, but certainly not least, the on the job knowledge an employee has leaves with them when they leave. So your customers will suffer as well even though they might not be aware of that.

Appearance

The word is not fair and customers are not fair either when it comes to their perceptions and opinions when it comes to how a person looks

The problem is that even though a perception can be 100% wrong, that perception IS the reality of the person who has it. They believe it and they act accordingly even though what they believe is the exact opposite of the truth.

There is a saying that goes "You only have one chance to make a good first impression." That means when someone sees you or meets you for the first time they will form an initial opinion on you. Over time that opinion is based more and more on reality but in the beginning, it is just a perception based on what someone was taught or has experienced.

When it comes to business, the owner must realize that their employees, especially the ones out on the floor or behind the counter, are the face of his franchise. The customers will look at the employee and form an opinion about the employee AND your business! Yes, the customer will form an opinion on your business based on the employees you hire! It is not fair and it is not accurate but it is human nature and there is not a damned thing you can do about it.

The key is to have employees who look and act like the customer expects them to look. Uniforms sometimes are used to assure a proper appearance clothing-wise. Some franchises will have rules like no facial hair, no hair below the shoulders, no facial piercings or tattoos or similar rules.

This is not done to discriminate against anyone but instead to have an appearance for your business that inspires confidence and trust in your business.

For example, if you own an auto repair franchise, you would expect to see a mechanic in jeans and a work shirt. You would not expect to see a mechanic come out from under your car in a three piece suit! But if you went to see a financial advisor in your bank and they came out in jeans and a work shirt, you would not be happy or inspired. You would expect the financial advisor to be dressed in a suit.

The point is to have your employees long and dress like they belong in that type of environment. You want to inspire confidence in the minds of your customers. You want them to feel at ease and comfortable in your store.

One last thing for some of our readers who might think that appearance has nothing to do with skill or ability. For those readers I will say that I agree with you. You are 100% right. How you look does not influence how skilled and able you are to do any job.

But also consider this important little fact. We are in business to make sales. So what you and I might feel is irrelevant. Your customers are the ones who decide where they do business and most of them are going to do business in places where they feel comfortable and at ease.

There are no laws that say that you customer must buy from your store. They can go wherever the heck they want to go.

And they will. So if you want to make sale, and if you want t make customers happy, give the customer what they want and expect from your business.

Employee Treatment

The last thing I want to talk about is how you treat your employees once you have hired them. You should realize that happy employees usually do more work and higher quality work than unhappy employees. So if you do things to make sure your employees know they are valued and appreciated, this is likely to improve the quality and amount of their work.

Employees should be treated as people and not possessions or slaves. They are deserving of your respect and should respect you as well. This means treating them like human beings and being aware of their needs and working conditions.

This does not mean you have to be their friend or invite them over to watch the game on Sundays. In fact, there should always be boundaries between owner and employees. You are their boss first and their friend second. You really should not blur those lines that much.

If those lines are not there your employees might try and take advantage of you or not do what they are supposed to do.

But a good owner or manager will try to do things to make working at the company better, easier and more enjoyable for employees. Staggering shifts to avoid peak travel times is something that doesn't cost much but can make people very happy. Accommodating a request or two every now and then to help an employee out is appreciated as well.

The employer – employee relationship is not just a one way arrangement. While the employee is hired to follow instructions and perform tasks, the employer cannot simply take and take and take and not give anything back other than their paycheck. Recognition, even if just simple "thank you" should be part of your business culture. When someone does something well, acknowledge it.

If someone should do something wrong or incorrectly or not according to policy, do not rant and rave. Instead, use it as a teaching opportunity and show them the right way to do it moving forward. If they still keep doing it wrong, then there will be time for yelling and screaming later on.

The key is to make coming to work as enjoyable and rewarding as possible.

You want to give employees reasons to want to stay with your company. You don't want to give them reasons to think about leaving. Once you do that, better opportunities arrive and your employees will start leaving and that will make you business suffer.

Your employees will be the life blood of your franchise business. Take time in finding and hiring the right employees and treat them well once you have them on board. You will find that spending time in this area will pay you and your business huge dividends down the road.

Focus on

Customer Satisfaction

There are many things to do when opening and growing your own business. There are building to construct, products to choose, stock and market and expenses to pay every month. Running a business can be complicated but some parts are really simple. In this chapter we are going to talk about one of the simpler things involved in your business.

We are going to talk about customer satisfaction.

Unless yours is a government office, or unless your product is something everyone must have and cannot get anywhere else, you must make your customers happy so that they continue to purchase your products and services. It is one of the most basic parts of every successful business. You need to keep customers coming back. If the customers don't come in or come back for more, your business is in trouble.

Look closely at the following true states regarding you and your business:

If your customers aren't happy, they won't purchase your products.

If your customers aren't happy they will find someplace else to go and buy what they need.

Without customers, there are no sales.

Without sales, there is no income.

Without income there are no profits.

Without income or profits the owner must pay salaries and other expenses out of pocket.

Without income the business fails and the owner goes to work for someone else asking if they want fries with their burger.

Ok, maybe the last one was a little dramatic but you get my overall point. Customers are the reason why businesses either fail or succeed. If a customer likes your business and feels they are treated right, they will come back.

If they feel the products and services you sell are of good quality, they will buy them. If they feel the prices you charge represent a good value for what they receive in return, they will continue to purchase them as long as they still want or need them.

If you look at successful businesses that are not the only source for a product or service, you will find that they routinely make their customers happy and satisfied. You will also find that their business model as well as their rules and procedures stress that as well. At the heart of every successful business is a focus on customer service.

Customer service involves a lot of common sense but also a lot of things most people never even think of when it come to making customers happy. This chapter is just a very high level overview on customer service and customer satisfaction. It should point you in the right direction and at least get you thinking about what you need to do regarding your business and making customers happy.

We suggest that you learn more about customer service and fortunately this is not a difficult or expensive thing to do. We highly recommend training manuals from The Customer Service Training Institute (www.infowhse.com). Their materials are excellent and very cost effective.

For now, here are a few things to keep in mind when it comes to your franchise business and customer satisfaction:

The Customer Service Chain

Customer service is more than just being pleasant to the customer and helping them make and complete their purchase. Many businesses feel that "service with a smile" is all that is needed to make people happy so they come back time and time again.

The fact is, that is just not the case. Everything from the time the customer walks through the door until they get home and unpack and use their purchase must go properly and positively to make the customer happy. If anything along the way should go wrong, you stand the chance of losing that customer.

Think of the total customer experience as a chain. Each point of the process is a link in that chain. Usual links might be the salesperson, price, billing, delivery, product quality, condition of the product when it is opened, and how the product performs when it is actually used. All of these, and probably more, are parts of the customer service chain. If any link breaks, the entire experience falls apart.

So if the salesperson is helpful and recommends the right product but the product is damaged or doesn't work when the customer gets it home, the experience has failed. If the product works perfectly but the billing department charges you twice or charges you the wrong price, the experience fails.

If the delivery truck is supposed to arrive between 9 and 11AM but it shows up at 4:4PM, the experience fails. In order for you to create a totally positive experience for the customer, every part of your business and sales process must work properly. I didn't say perfectly because people do make mistakes, but the processes should work properly and be customer friendly and the product should be of high quality.

Anything less is courting disaster.

Everyone Should be Trained

Hopefully we all agree now that every part of our business is involved in customer satisfaction. Now that we understand this we should also agree that we should provide every employee in our business training and direction on how to best serve our customers. In other words, we need everyone on the same page when it comes to what we want our customers to experience when they walk through the doors or pick up the phone.

There are several ways to give your employees this training. The source we listed above has some great manuals that cover just about every aspect of customer service. You don't have to send people to costly seminars or have them take long college courses. That level of education at this point is not required.

But all employees should be given the background they need to start thinking in terms of the customer and not just the business. This change in thinking is critical.

Don't fall into the trap of thinking that only some employees need to think about the customers. That is the way many businesses fall short of creating the very best customer service experience for their customers.

The Customer Doesn't Care About Your Policies or Procedures

Here is something most business owners and employees just don't realize. Your customers don't give a damn about your policies, procedures or limitations. If something doesn't allow them to get what they want, they do not care about it. Your problems are your problems and not your customers. Once you understand that, you tend to look at things a little bit differently.

Every business needs policies and procedures in order for their business to function properly and consistently. Without a structured way of doing business every customer would receive a different type or level of treatment and some would get treated better or worse than the next customer. This can lead to customer confusion and frustration.

Most of the time a business will look at their policies and procedure and evaluate them on how well they serve the business. Do they help solve a problem or help the business become more successful or profitable? If the answer is "YES!" then the policy stays. If the answer is no the policy goes.

But well run and customer focused businesses look at their policies, procedures and rules from the customer's point of view as well. If something is unfair to the customers, they look for ways to change things so they can better serve their customers. Even if the cost to the business is a little bit higher, they realize the value of a satisfied customer is worth the added expense. This is a long range view of things

As you start your business, evaluate your policies and procedures and make sure they are fair to your customers as well. An important part of every customer experience revolves around whether or not the customer feels they were treated fairly or not. If you make your policies fair, customer will appreciate it.

Here's an example:

Your refund policy is now 30 days if accompanied by a receipt. No receipt, no refund. This protects your business against unwanted returns and products not sold by your business. But it might not be seen as fair by your customers.

So you do a little research and find that other businesses offer 60 days. Plus, your system allows you to access customer purchases by their name and phone number. So you can change the policy to a straight 60 days with or without a receipt as long as the customer is listed in your database.

This helps the customer who might have lost or thrown out their receipt and also gives them a longer period of time to request a refund. Your customers will appreciate this and find doing business with you more fair and more enjoyable.

The policy might cost your business a little bit more in additional returns but at the same time it will make it more customer friendly which should result in more repeat customers and more new customers.

Keep it Positive

Stay away from negative words, phrases and statements. Customers do not care about what you can't do. They want to know what you can do. So say "Mr. Smith, what I can do for you is….." That is more positive and will probably be received a lot better in the mind of the customers.

Approach everything from the positive point of view. People sometimes shut down when they hear something negative. People who approach everything from the positive point of view are usually more successful in making customers happy.

Meeting Expectations is Not Good Enough

This is another huge misconception by many businesses. Giving a customer what they expect does not impress them. They can probably get what they expect in 5 or 10 places around town. What you need to give your customers is MORE than what they expect. When you do that, the customer stops for a moment and is impressed because they received more than what they thought they would. That is always a much better way to serve a customer.

That is why it is important that your business provides more than what your competition provides to their customers. You want customers to flock to your business because they know they will be treated better and be given for value for their money than they would anywhere else. If you just provide what everyone else does, your customer might go to your competition because they are closer or more convenient.

You need to give your customers solid reasons to come into your business instead of someone else's. You have to treat them better, provide more value and do other things they don't expect you to do. It doesn't have to be anything huge that you offer that is different than anywhere else but it needs to be something that your customers attach value to.

That might be longer or more convenient hours, value added services such as free warranty extensions or credit or maybe free delivery. It is not so much what the add-on costs you but what the customer feels it is worth to them that matters.

Be Helpful but not Smothering

Sometimes you can walk around a store for hours and not see a single employee or find someone to help you. Then you leave and go somewhere else where you are continually asked if you need help and are just not allowed to shop in peace. Though these are the two extremes, both of them are wrong in the eyes of the customer.

Customers want to be helped when they need it and they also want to be left alone to shop or browse in peace. Sometimes it is difficult to know what a particular customer is looking for when they come in but you can make it easier on both you and them.

Greet your customer when they enter the store and ask them if they want or need help. If they do, then help them. If they say "No" then wish them well and tell them to come to you if they have any questions or need anything. Then leave them alone.

If you have to make an error in judgment when it comes to helping a customer, it is always better to greet them and ask them if they need help when you think they need it. Walking around looking for someone to help you or feeling ignored is never a good thing for any customer.

Make Things Easy to Find

Have you ever walked into a store trying to find something and find the store has little or no organization and that everything is really difficult to find? Nothing is where you think it would be and you had a hard time finding anything.

When you design or lay out your selling floor, make things easy to find and make it enjoyable and attractive to the customer. Let them enjoy the process instead of getting frustrated. After all, some people just want to come in, get what they want or need, and get back to their lives. Do your best to make that possible.

Be Knowledgeable

We already discussed why you should have product knowledge when it comes to things you sell or to the interests that your business caters to. Some customers will come in for advice and you should be able to provide it to them

Every employee doesn't have to be an expert on every product, but at any given time there should be someone knowledgeable available to answer questions and recommend the proper products.

Many customers will remain loyal to the businesses that help them get things done and solve their problems. Many people will pay more for the same products they could get cheaper elsewhere because of the help and assistance they get from businesses such as yours. Anything that makes your customers life easier or better is something they will appreciate from you and your business.

Follow-Up

Customer service does not stop after the sale is made. Depending on your business you might want to follow up after purchases are made. For example, if you sell coffee you would call a customer after they buy a cup of coffee to make sure it was good. But if you sold a car or a television, a follow-up phone call to see if the customer had any questions or encountered any problems might be appreciated by the customer.

Follow-up calls might also be used to sell value added services like warranties or accessories but always made that secondary in relation to making sure the customer is satisfied with their purchase.

Handle Problems Quickly and Fairly

Even the best run businesses with the highest quality products and very best employees will have mistakes happen or products fail. It is not so much if these things are going to happen but rather when they will happen. It is what your business does when problems occur that can help or hurt your business.

There have been many times when a problem creates an angry customer but the business handles the issue so well they turn the angry customer into a customer for life. It is all about what happens when the customer brings the problem to your attention that can make all the difference in the world.

There are two factors that come into play when problems occur. The first is the time required to resolve the issue. This time frame should be as short as possible. If the time to resolve drags out longer than expected, the customer will get angrier and it will cost you more to make them happy again. So once you are aware of a problem, move heaven and earth to resolve it quickly.

The second factor is how you resolve the problem. If you only watch out for the interests of the business in your resolution then you might create an even angrier customer in the process.

The best way to resolve problems is by giving the customer as much of what they want or need while at the same time addressing the interests of the business.

Problem resolution is a very interesting process and I would strongly advise you to read up on this part of business. Sometimes a few extra dollars spent on a customer today giving them more than they expected can pay huge dividends to you in the near future. Do not look at resolving problems as a win-lose battle but rather as a win-win process where the interests of both parties are addressed fairly.

The Value of Repeat Customers

Repeat customers are important to every business because repeat customers are almost "free" to the businesses they patronize. Regular or first time customers come in as a result of advertising, marketing and promotion. So the customer that come in as a result of advertising and marketing cost the business money to bring them through the doors.

Repeat customers, on the other hand, come back because the experience was positive and they feel they got great value from their past experience.

While it might have cost the business money to bring them through the doors the first time, every other time they come in it was because of their previous experience and not marketing or advertising.

New customers are expensive. Every business needs new customer because every business loses customers each and every year even though they might be doing everything perfectly. Each year a percentage of customers will move, pass away, or no longer need the products and services they had been purchasing. Regardless of the reason that your customers are no longer buying from you, the effect on your sales is the same.

So business must continue to promote and advertise to replace customers who no longer walk in through the doors. This includes angry customers as well. The more customers that leave the business the more customers the business will have to replace. So it is in the best interest of every business to keep their customers coming back time and time again for more purchases and more sales.

Imagine how much more difficult it would be if your business had to bring in new customers for every sales they make. Some businesses might be in this position because of the nature of the products they sell but most businesses rely on repeat business.

Even those businesses who sell once in a lifetime purchases rely on their customers spreading the word and recommending your business to their family and friends. So an argument could be made that even though the original customer is not walking through your doors new customer that they referred are.

The point here is that every successful business needs repeat customers and repeat business from those customers. Therefore we must make every effort to keep existing customers happy so they can come back again and gain. Here is an eye opening statistic: Surveys have shown that it can cost a business up to 10 times more to bring a new customer through the doors than it costs them to keep an existing customer happy.

I'm no accountant but even that opens my eyes just a little bit wider. Take care of your existing customers and they will help take care of you and your business. Make them happy and they will come back. Give them more than what they expect and they will come back. Show that you care about your customers and they will remain loyal to you even though your products might be able to be purchased elsewhere for less.

Take care of your customers. Any other approach will almost definitely lead to disaster.

Know Your Competition

Just like sports team scout their opponents before they play them, business owners must also "scout" their competition both before they open and after they establish their business in the community. No one business operates in a vacuum so it is important to know and understand what your competition is doing.

As we have already stated, good businesses provide more than other similar businesses in the area. The "more" might mean lower prices, better selection, value added services, better hours and a host of other things customer place a high value on. But the only way you can be sure that you are providing an overall greater value is to know what the competition offers their customers.

Before deciding on your franchise and desired location, scope out the area. Visit the stores you identify as your competition and see what they offer to their customers. If you honestly feel that you can do better and offer more to your customers, that is a positive sign that your business will have a chance to do very well in the area. After all, most customers will do business where they feel they get the most from their experience.

But if there is competition that offers a great deal to their customers now, and you don't feel you are in the position to offer at least that let alone more right now, that might be a sign that tells you to choose another business or a different location. Established businesses usually have higher cash flow and are able to afford to offer good and services that new businesses cannot afford. If you find yourself in that position, re-evaluate whether or not you can compete.

Be honest in that evaluation and do not fool yourself into believing that people will come to you because of your sparkling personality or charming wit. Trust me when I say they will not. Your customers will come to you only if you offer something they need and their overall experience is better than your competition. Personality will help, and your charming wit might make the customers smile, but you have to at least match, and hopefully exceed what others are providing to their customers.

Check out things like refund policies, store hours, product selection, delivery options, service plans, installation if applicable and anything else that customers will purchase your kind of services need or would appreciate. Then, look at your business and see how it compares to the other businesses in town or within your area. If anything appears to be less than what the others are offering, see how feasible it might be to change your business model to make your business more appealing to the customer.

It is also important that you understand that this is an on-going process. It is not a one-time task that you are done with forever. Keep in mind that the other businesses also are in the process of making THEIR businesses the best in town as well. If they are not, you are in luck, but most of them will be interested in their future success as you are.

I would make keeping aware of your competition a continual process where you constantly watch advertising, window signs, listen to customer comments and just being aware of what is going on with the competition. There is always the chances that your business will offer something more or better than they do and that you will steal customers away from t=other businesses. So they are likely to notice and will scope out your business to see where their customers are going.

When they see that your prices are lower or your services are better, they will do the same thing you would do. They would stop and see how they could improve their business to bring their customers back. So what your competition was doing last month might not be what they are doing this month. The only way for you to keep your business on top is to know what your competition is doing at all times.

There are services that offer people to visit businesses you select in your area and give you a report on what they are doing and their overall appeal in comparison to other businesses and yours. These kinds of "secret shoppers" are useful because they have an unbiased view of the businesses and will not have an ego that insists their business is the best when it really isn't. Sometimes this can really help a business keep on the right track. But understand that there is a cost to this service.

The other option is that you make these visits yourself and see for yourself what is really going on. If time is not a huge issue I recommend that you make the first couple of visits at least because you can get a first-hand look at their layout, product selection, customer service and other things that you might really like and want to institute in your business. A "secret shopper" might not report of those things.

When it comes to making changes in your business to make it better or more appealing to your customers, make sure to get any change approved by the parent company. Always remember that although this is your business, you have agreed to stay within the boundaries of the franchise agreement. Since continuity of experience is extremely important for all franchises, they may have strict rules on what can or can't be changed.

On the other hand, franchises are always looking to make their brand stronger and more valuable. If you spot something great, or have a great idea of your own, bring it to the parent company. They might see the value and potential behind this idea and allow you to test it with the intention of bringing that change to all locations. This is one of the ways brands and businesses evolve.

All in all if you just understand that all businesses constantly jockey back and forth for sales and market share, you will understand the continual need to have your finger on the pulse of your business and the others in town. This is not a complicated process or a time consuming one. A visit to each of your competition might take you 10 minutes or maybe a few minutes more if it is a huge store.

The first visit will take the longest because you will be seeing everything for the first time and there might be a lot to remember. Get yourself a binder and create a folder for each of your competition. Write down important facts about each competitor such as hours, refund policies, warranties, added services, delivery costs, etc. This knowledge will help you plan your business more accurately.

Last but not least, there is another important reason to know what your competition is doing. That is because many customers will try to lie to get something cheaper or get something they are not entitled to.

For example, you might have a customer come up to you and tell you that XYZ appliance delivers their machines for free while you charge $50. You can reply that you know XYZ charges $75 to deliver to their area because you constantly check to make sure you have the lowest prices and the best services. Usually that is enough to shut the customer down. But if they insist, keep in mind that XYZ just might have offered free delivery to steal some of your sales away from you!

That's why knowing your competition is an ongoing and extremely important process for all businesses that have any kind of competition. Which almost definitely includes you and your business.

Get Involved in the Community

Part of the success of any business is having the public become aware of your presence in the area and developing a positive feeling or impression of you and your business. One way to accomplishing both of these objectives is by making sure to get your business involved in your community.

That means showing up at events, sponsoring events and becoming involved in civic groups and charitable organizations. That might mean donating products or money, giving your time or both. Anything you and your business can do to expose your business to the general public will help establish your new business in the community.

Think of becoming involved in the community as a two sided approach. First, being part of good civic events that help individuals or groups is always a great thing to do whether you do it as an individual or as a business. We all donate time and money towards the things that touch us and as a businessman you should do the same on behalf of your business.

Second, if doing something just because you feel it's right or because you want to doesn't appeal to you, think about sponsorship and donating products or money as just another type of advertising expense.

So instead of buying an ad, you sponsor an event and get a banner put up with your business featured on it or maybe even an ad or mention in the program. You might even get television coverage and have your business name shown on the local or regional news. This will help your business in two ways.

First, the exposure your banner gets means more people will see your business name and logo. Even if they are not aware of it, their brains will process that image and it will seem more familiar to them. If they don't know of your business, this might make them curious. If they are aware of your business this added impression will help them remember.

Since repetition of advertising is important, any exposure your business gets will help convince people to walk through your doors the next time they need what you are selling.

Second, you and your business will get recognition as being a supporter of certain charities or cause. A LOT of people make it a point to support those businesses that support the same things they believe in. So supporting your local church might increase the number or parishioners that go to that church becoming your customers. Supporting a local charity will help bring in supporters of that charity as well. The more groups and associations that you support the larger the potential group of new customers might be.

On a higher level, there are a lot of people who believe in giving back to those who give to their community. So if they see your business logo up there on the sponsor list, they just might go to your store over the store they currently use. People like to take care of the local guys instead of some of the large "big box" stores that come in and drive everyone else out. So getting involved on a local level and giving back to the community can help in that regard as well.

Here are a few ideas on how your business can use community involvement to help others while growing your business:

Sponsorship

Why not make your business synonymous with a certain event or event in your local area? You might even get your business name in the event name such as "The 2nd Annual Herb's Burgers Town Marathon". Even if your name isn't part of the event name, having your business banner raised high or your name on the program or T-Shirt can work wonders!

Fundraisers

Why not offer to donate a percentage of your sales over a certain time to a specific organization? This way you make sales so your contribution is really paid by the community. As long as you break even, it won't cost you a penny. You might even make a profit on those sales which truly makes this a win-win for everyone!

Support

Find ways to support programs and organizations that are important to your community. Pick the ones that are the most highly respected. Being associated with the best makes people think your business is the best!

Churches

Purchase an Ad in the church bulletin or newspaper. These ads are inexpensive and a lot of people read them and appreciate the support for their church.

Donate

Sometimes you can get involved without a cash donation or giving any time. If you sell products or services, why not consider donating a prize to a raffle. If your business cleans houses, for example, offer a free house cleaning as one of the prizes. The people buy tickets that support the organization and the winner gets a free house cleaning. An added benefit is that you just might do a great job and impress the person so much they hire your business to come back every week to clean their house!

Another way to donate is whenever you hear of someone in the community that has been hit hard by something in life and that could use your products or services to help make their lives a little bit better. For example, you might donate the materials to build a wheel chair ramp for a returning veteran or someone who was paralyzed in a car accident. Or you could donate clothing and supplies to victims of a house fire. If you see someone with a need and you can help, then do it. It's just the right thing to do.

I urge everyone who starts a new business, or even has an existing business, to get involved as much as they can with their local community and the organizations that reside there. Help one another and help those who are unable to help themselves. Not only is this the right and moral thing to do, it will also help your business grow and get a wonderfully positive reputation at the same time.

But be careful when it comes to soliciting new business at the same time. If you turn volunteering or donating into a sales pitch, it can really upset some people and ruin the gesture and the desired result. Place your focus on the event and the organization or people you are helping and leave the sales pitch at the door. While there is nothing wrong with benefitting from your actions, the primary focus and motivation should be from helping others and not from pitching for new business.

Cash Flow

While every business needs to be concerned with cash flow, start-ups or younger businesses need to be especially concerned with where their money goes after it comes in. How we handle our finances in those first months or years could very well mean the difference between a successful business and an early bankruptcy.

Almost every business has a period when it first starts where sales are not enough to sustain the business. When you open your doors that first day, you might only get a trickle of sales or you might get a windfall depending on the advanced promotion and your franchise brand. But let's all agree that it will take a little time for sales to get where they are going to eventually be if you do things right.

In those early months, it is important that the business owner knows to the penny how much is coming in and how much is going out.

We should spend enough to properly operate and market our business but not spend money on other non-essential expenses until sales are stabilized.

Depending on the area and the type of business you operate, you will never be able to understand your sales patterns until at least two years, sometimes more, have passed. For example, if you open a business in September and do really well through March, that's great. But you still will not know how sales will be in the warmer weather or during different times of the year. Some products and areas have huge variations in sales and population.

When this happens to be the case, you might think you are making money hand over fist for a few months but then people close their homes for the summer or winter and sales drop off. Or maybe you sell ice cream and do great from May to October and then sell very little November through April.

You need to understand this so that you can take steps to make sure your business has the resources and cash flow to sustain it year round. If you see $10,00 a month for 6 months and then sell nothing for the next 6 months, that averages out to $5,000 a month. So you can't spend at the $10,000 a month rate during those 6 months because if you do, you will have nothing left to pay expenses and bill for those other 6 months.

Consult with your accountant on what is a prudent budget and approach for your area and your type of business. Follow his recommendations to the letter. If you want to be more frugal, that might be a good thing as long as you still spend to promote your business. Do not be so frugal that you stop advertising and promoting your business to the people in your area. Just make sure everything you spend money on is needed and justified.

Another aspect concerning cash flow is the salary or money the owner takes out of the business every week or month. Some owners draw a specific amount each month while others might pay expenses, set aside some funds for next month and take the rest. Discuss the best option with your accountant.

But you might be better off planning on taking no money out of the business for the first few months just to make sure the business can sufficiently sustain itself. You need to make this decision up front as this would affect the amount of capital you need going into the business. Not drawing any money from the business for several months would require that you have more money saved up in the beginning. After all, you will still have your own personal expenses.

The key to all of this is financial awareness.

Making sure the business has money to sustain itself through the start-up process is critical to your long term growth and success. Understanding what your sales will be over the course of a full year will help you decide on how much you will need to sustain the business and how much you will be able to safely and responsibly take out of the business for your own use.

Also understand that this is an on-going process. Current sales are not a guarantee of future sales. Sales of one month will not always be the same as another month. But if you plan, and if you remain aware, both you and your business will become more successful for a longer period of time.

Talk about this in depth with your accountant and financial advisor. A little consultation now will help you make better and more informed decisions later. Plus, it will save you a lot of time, heartache and money when you do things right the first time.

Networking

Just about everyone needs help at one time or another. Also, just about everyone makes mistakes every now and then and those mistakes can set you back time and money. So it makes sense to seek out help, get other points of view and most important, learn from the successes and mistakes of others.

Networking is a fancy term for listening to and talking with others. These can be other franchise owners, business owners from your community, people on online forums and even people who walk in off the street that have some particular area of expertise.

It is a very foolish man who refuses to listen to other people. It is a clueless man who thinks he knows everything about everything.

It is a stupid man who thinks no one can teach him anything about anything. So don't be foolish, clueless or stupid. Seek out and listen to other people at every opportunity.

In the franchise environment, a huge potential source of information and assistance might lie with other franchise owners. Especially when those owners are outside of your local area and do not view your location as a threat to their well being. But being able to talk to other owners who sell the same products and services using the same business model can be very helpful.

If your franchise holds owners meetings, then attend them and questions but also listen to the other questions and the answers. If someone brings up something chances are you have encountered the same problem or situation yourself and can either benefit from the answer or be part of the solution.

Another source of help would be local associations or organizations that pertain to your particular industry or product type. There are all kind of organizations for every market and every area. Belonging to these associations not only allow you to build relationships with others but also get up to the minute information on your area and industry. This information can be critical to the success of your business.

Civic and government associations are also useful in learning about your area and industry. Relationships in these areas can help you identify possible ways to get your business known and recognized within your community. They can also help you by being the voice of your business when it comes to rules and regulations and other government or tax issues. Never under estimate the value of relationships in this area!

Business owners should try to put themselves out there in the community and form relationships with other business owners as well as the people who live, work and play in that area. The more you and your business become known, the larger your potential customer base might become.

I would caution you when it comes to networking that you do not turn your networking into a sales pitch. Keep it on an informational basis with the intent on helping each other and not soliciting new business. That is liable to turn people off and you might find yourself not welcome at future meetings or events.

Time Management

One of the most difficult parts of running your own business, especially in the beginning, is finding the time to do everything that has to be done while making sure that you do everything the right way. Sometimes this is a daunting task as it can seem that there is just too much to be done and far too little time in which to do it.

There are several things a business owner can do to make it easier for them to handle the everyday chores and responsibilities of running their own business. While this is not an all inclusive list of suggestions, it is a good start that can at least help you start thinking in a more efficient and organized manner.

Get Organized

So much time is wasted looking for things that aren't where they should be or doing things in a haphazard manner.

Organize your business and office so that you know where everything is and when everything needs to get done.

You simply cannot "fly by the seat of your pants" and expect things to magically fall into place when you need them to. When you control the process and when you schedule your time you will get far more done in less time and usually get better results. When you are running around trying to figure out what to do next your business will control you instead of you controlling your business.

A system, no matter how simple, that allows you to know where things are and when things need to be done will pay your huge dividends every month. The result is less time wasted looking or searching for things and more time spent growing your business or spending time with your family. It just makes no sense to take 3 hours to do a one hour task.

Know What Needs to Be Done

The key to properly managing your time is to first know what needs to be done, how often it needs to be done and when it needs to be done. Some things, such as financial statements and reports, need to be done at the same time every month to insure accuracy of certain data.

Daily reports must be done at the same time of the day to insure accuracy and for comparison purposes. Monthly reports should be done at the same time of the month for the same reason.

Sometimes when you are running a business the little things often get forgotten. But even these little things can be very important. We take some things, especially those things that are going well, for granted and sometimes forget all about them until they get neglected to the point that they cause problems. By that time we could have a real problem on our hands that will take even more time to resolve.

The best thing to do when you first get started is make list of everything, no matter how trivial or small, that needs to get done and how often each thing needs to get done. This will give you a list of tasks that you can schedule so that everything gets done when it needs to be and in an organized manner.

Once you know everything that needs to be done, you can start creating a schedule that will allow you to get everything done in an organized manner so that nothing is neglected or done incorrectly.

Don't Neglect or Procrastinate

When things get hectic or busy, we tend to put some things off so that we can do other things right this moment.

While that is an effective strategy as we soon will discuss, the problem lies when we put things off for so long that they never get done at all.

Procrastination can really damage your business and reduce your profits. Certain tasks need to be done regularly or your business will suffer. For example, you might hate to do inventory so you put it off and you put it off. The next thing you know someone comes in to buy something and you are all out because you never ordered it! Operate your business by making one simple commitment. That is to do everything when it is supposed to be done and not when you feel like it or have the time.

You will never have the time if you wait for when you have the time. You will always have the time when you control how you schedule your time. A time for everything and everything done on time is the only way to run your business.

Prioritize

Even though many things need to be done at the same time, certain things will be more important than others and should be done first. For example, placing cash in the register before the store opens would be more important than refilling the napkin holders. We want to make sure the really important things get done first so they will not negatively impact our business.

Other things need to be done in a certain sequence in order to be done properly or to give the most accurate results. For example, you would count the money in the register before you take it out and send it off to the bank at closing time. If you sent it off to the bank first, you wouldn't know how many of each bill you sent out. Just like you put your underwear on first and then your pants. You would look pretty silly if you did it the other way around!

Make a list of everything that has to be done. Rank every item on the list as to its importance and when it has to be done. If something needs to be done before or after something else, indicate that as well. Then take the items on your list and move them over to another list that has them all in the order in which they need or should be done.

The idea behind this is to create an orderly way of approaching things. Sometimes we might just not have the time we need to do everything and it is critical that the really important things get done first. That doesn't mean we forget about the other things, it just means we need to spend what little time we have to get the most important stuff done!

Schedule Time

If you don't schedule your time properly you will never have enough time to do what you need to get done.

I am a big fan of "to do" lists and use one almost every day. I create them the night before and add to them throughout the day if something else should pop up during the day. It is amazing how much more you can get done when you have that list in front of you.

Some of the things we need to do are "quick hitters" that can be done very quickly. It will shock you how many of these things you can get done in very little time if you are just reminded of them throughout the day. You will look at your list and be surprised to see 9 things crossed off of it and it is still mid morning! Without the list little things get forgotten or lost as other things that are happening take your mind off them.

Another benefit of the list is that you can see what is left over at the end of the day and you can transfer those items over to the next day. This helps keep things from getting really backed up and forgotten.

Another effective strategy is to create a week's worth of lists at the same time. What this allows you to do is balance out your days so that no single day is jammed packed with things to do while another day is almost empty. We all know things pop up from time to time and throw our schedules off. If our schedule is balanced at the beginning of the week, we will stand a better chance of still getting things done even despite the unexpected interruptions and changes.

Believe me when I say that if you do not schedule your time you will find yourself spending more time getting less done. You will find yourself hurrying and panicking to try and get everything done because you just were not organized. Don't let the task schedule you, you schedule the task. Things work so much better that way!

Delegate

No one has ever said that we have to do all the work ourselves. Granted, there are some things we will want to do ourselves for security or privacy reasons, or maybe because we possess a special set of skills that are required to complete the task properly. But some things can be done by others once they are given proper instruction or training.

Delegating is one way that you can get more things done in less time and utilize the skills of others to lessen your work load. For example, you might take on the task of counting the money and closing out the register while one of your employees locks the doors and secures the perimeter. Or maybe a few employees replenish the supplies that will be needed for the morning rush.

You will probably be able to look at your list of things that have to be done and find at least a few that can be done by other people

You can keep the critical or financially related tasks to yourself if that makes you feel more comfortable but everything else should be up for discussion.

Keep in mind that when you ask someone else to do something that you need to provide training, direction and specific instructions the first couple of times the person does that task. You cannot expect someone to do something exactly like you want it done if you don't take the time to train them on the specifics first!

It is also a great idea to do the task with the other person the first time or two. The first time show them how to do it and give them specific instructions. The next time, stand by them while they do it and point out things they should be doing if they are not doing them. Then, if you are comfortable, you can turn them loose and let them do things by themselves. Just be patient because other people are not exactly like you and may take a little bit longer to get the knack of how you want things done.

Delegation is a very effective way of utilizing the talents of different people to get as much done as possible in the least amount of time. Delegation frees the owners up to spend more time running and growing the business while giving the employees more responsibility and a feeling that they are contributing to the success of the business as well.

When done properly, delegation provides a win-win resolution for everyone when it comes to getting stuff done.

Sub Contract

Sometimes there might be things that need to be done that we just don't have the time or the skills to do ourselves and neither do our employees. In those cases, we might want to look into sub-contracting out the work to people that have the time and/or the skills to do it faster and better.

Maybe we hire a bookkeeper to do our books and handle our payroll each week. Instead of mowing the grass in front of the store ourselves we might hire a landscaper to do that for us. Maybe even hire a company to handle our quarterly inventory for us instead of working an overnight or closing early one day to do it ourselves.

Even though there are costs incurred in having other people do work that we might be able to do ourselves, we can sometimes save money by having others do those things for us. Sometimes we can dedicate time to do more cost effective things ourselves and have the less costly things done by others.

For example, if you produce the products or services that you sell and you earn $50 an hour when doing so, it makes no sense for you to mow the lawn when a landscaper can do it for $25.

That is because in the hour it would take to mow the lawn, you could earn $50 while paying out only $25. There are many other tasks that could fall into this situation as well.

Your time and resources should be directed at the things that you do best and that pay you the greatest dividends. Put your skills and time where they pay you the most and let everyone else do the other stuff. It just makes sense.

Last, but certainly not least, time management helps you avoid burnout. Burnout occurs when too much time and efforts over longer periods of time decreases your ability to function at your best. Though people can be expected to "step it up" for short periods of time such as when people are out sick or on vacation, expecting someone to do the work of two people for longer periods of time is just foolish and unrealistic.

Your goals should be to use your time efficiently and profitably while living a balanced life at the same time. That means spending time not only in and on your business but also with your family and other areas of your personal life as well. This enables you to continue functioning at a high level while everything around you gets done properly and effectively.

It's not all that difficult. It just takes a little bit of practice. So start making your lists and adding some structure into your life today. Remember that there is no better time to start than right now. Because if you don't change anything, nothing will change.

And that, my friends, would be a huge waste of time.

Dealing with Perception

If I were to tell you that you had to deal with the actual performance of your business and the reputation it created, you would have no problem with that. After all, it just makes sense to accept the responsibility for your actions and what you created. But how would you feel if I told you that you also had to deal with what people *thought* about your business as well. That you would also have to deal with what people thought whether it were true or not.

Well, that is exactly what I am telling you. Not only do business owners have to concern themselves with the actual performance and reputation of their business but they also have to concern themselves against rumors, gossip and other perceptions even if they are far from the truth.

Consider this for a moment. If someone believes that your business treats their customers poorly and because of that feeling they buy from someone else, does it really make any difference whether that perception is right or wrong?

Either way it costs you sales. Either way the person might repeat that feeling to other people because he or she believes it to be true.

The reality of it is that someone's perception IS their reality. If I believe something is true I will act and respond like it is true until someone or something proves to me that I am wrong. If I believe a business takes advantage of their customers or sells inferior products, I am not likely to give that business the benefit of the doubt. Instead, I will probably look elsewhere to make my purchases.

One of the most difficult things for any business to do is overcome a poor or negative perception. Studies have shown that it can take as many as 10 positive experiences to counter the effects of just one bad experience. That means once a customer perceives your business to be lacking in something, you will have to impress them the next 10 times by doing everything perfectly! Not just the next time or the next 2 or 3 times but up to 10 times to wipe out that one bad experience.

Because of this, the most efficient way to deal with a bad perception is to not let that bad perception gain a foothold at all. Your efforts should always be focused on producing a level of customer service and customer experience that would be so positive that the occasional poor experience would not have any effect at all.

We should want to have a reputation that is so strong and so positive that when a disgruntled customer says anything bad about your business people will not accept it or believe it, they will come to your defense. That should be our ultimate goal. To produce disciples for our brand and our business.

You cannot stop people from saying bad things. There will always be people with over the top expectations that will go on a rampage when they don't get everything exactly as they want it. There will always be people you cannot make happy no matter what great lengths you go to in trying. Angry customers are a part of every business and every industry. Our goal is not to eliminate them because that will never happen.

But we can limit their effectiveness by making our business bullet-proof. We want to make sure customers feel so strongly positive about us and our business that the angry people just don't stand a chance. We do this by exceeding the expectations of the customer and giving them the very best experience we possibly can.

That means establishing a reputation as a customer friendly and fair minded business. It means having policies and rules that are customer friendly and fair to both the customer and the business.

It is all about giving the customer the benefit of the doubt and being liberal in dealing with customers and their requests.

Think about how you might feel about a business that treated you very well after you had a problem. Maybe you had a defective product and lost the receipt and the business took the product back even though there was no receipt. You would probably have felt pretty good about the business at that moment. But if the business held firm to their no refunds without a receipt policy, you would have been upset even though it was you that lost the receipt. Again, fault and right or wrong doesn't enter into things here. It is strictly the perception of whether you and your business were helpful or not that matters.

Taking this example one step further, what was the final cost to the business when the return was accepted? Nothing. The manufacturer or distributor would have issued a credit or provided a free replacement. Granted there would have been some record keeping and handling involved but those expenses are trivial. But at the end of the day, we had a very happy customer and not an angry one.

Take a close look at every part of your business. Ask yourself is there anything that could provide any kind of negative perception in the mind of the customer?

Is your advertising misleading or just designed to get people through your doors? Are your employees more interested in earning a commission or really helping the customer? Is your store neat and clean and customer friendly?

Do your policies and procedures favor the store or are they fair for all concerned? Are they too restrictive? How do they compare to other businesses in the area? That is important because your business will be compared to the others in the area. Based on that comparison a perception will be made. It is up to you whether that perception will be a negative one or a positive one.

Do yourself a favor and create as many a positive perception as you possibly can. That will only serve to help you and your business in the future.

The Uniform Level of Experience

A major part of what you purchased when you joined the franchise is the type of experience that customers seem to expect from your brand name. The franchise is based on the premise that regardless of where the customer finds one of the franchises, they will get the same experience, similar product selection and quality. It makes little difference where the franchise is located because the customer will be treated the same way at every location.

That means that the family from the South who is vacationing in the West can stop into a franchise location and get the same quality of products and services that they could buy at home. There is no guesswork and nothing to risk.

It should be understood that if you see the franchise logo, you know what you are going to get when you order it. If this is not the case then the franchise brand loses value.

This kind of uniform customer experience is built into the franchise model that you purchased. The method that is used to design, implement and operate the franchise is designed to replicate the same experience over and over and over again regardless of location or surroundings.

One of the problems that some franchises have are owners that do not adhere to the business model or make changes in how the customer is treated or which products they receive. While they might do this with the best intentions, any deviation from the standard way of doing business can negatively affect the franchise brand.

For example, if you buy into a burger franchise and change the type of meat that is used or the way that it's cooked, you may produce a burger that is either better or worse than what is produced at other locations. Strange as it may seem even something better can spell real trouble for every franchise owner. In fact anything that alters the level of expectations with the customer spells trouble for the franchise.

For example, using the same burger example, if your changes produce a better burger, customers are going to expect that same burger quality at other location when they travel. They will be unhappy when they don't get it and that is bad for all the other owners. There will now be confusion as far as the brand in the mind of the customers. Why is the burger at one location better than the others? Which one is the right one? What should I expect next time?

If you produce an inferior burger then customers might not go to another location in fear of getting another low quality burger there as well. Some people refuse to give anything another try after they have been burned just once. So your poor quality burger can effect sales at all the other locations and not just yours.

In order for the franchise brand to remain strong and powerful, it must be a product that is delivered over and over again in the exact same way with the same level of quality no matter where the product is purchased. It is not up to the franchisee to decide which is better or worse. It is up to the parent company and any changes should be rolled out company-wide and not just to one area or one location. Care must be taken to insure that everyone, everywhere get the same type and quality of food.

Most people like what they are familiar with. If you are in another area and need something, chances are you will look for someplace familiar to get it. You will pass up the local mom and pop stores and head over to the better known franchise because you have a level of familiarity and security in that particular brand. In other words, you know what you are going to receive when you walk through the doors. As long as you get that, everything is good. If you don't get what you expect, everything can go bad.

Franchise owners must be loyal to each other and not try to change their business at the expense of the other owners. If changes need to be made, they should be introduced through the company and field tested in smaller areas until proven. If everything works out great then they can be rolled out company-wide so every customer can benefit while retaining the franchise brand and uniform level of service.

Another important reason to follow the rules and business model to the letter is that often franchisees can lose their franchises if they do not follow procedure and create a different experience for the customer. This is important because when you buy a franchise you are buying the brand and the brand recognition. If anything should happen to devalue that brand. Every owner, as well as the parent company will suffer.

So if you deviate too much from the model, you could lose everything. Your initial investment and the rights to continue selling the products and services and the right to use the brand name.

Here are just a few of the things that customers come to expect when it comes to visiting a franchise out of their local area:

Appearance

Your building, logo and overall appearance must be the same, or at least extremely similar, to the other locations. Otherwise the customer might be confused and unsure that you are really part of the company or just a private business using a similar logo in order to confuse the customer. Sometimes building might not be an issue but signage and logos must be exact replicas of the ones currently being used.

Product Selection

People visit franchises because the products and services appeal to them on some level. Most customers have one or two "favorites" that they purchase when they come into the store. They like the same food item, the same drink or they like a certain service that the location offers.

When they go into a different location they have the expectation that those same products and services will be offered there as well. If they do not see what they came in for they will be disappointed and consider the visit a negative experience.

The core products offered by the franchise must be available in all locations to insure brand continuity. There might be slight local differences like a couple of area favorites or region specific offerings but the main line of products and service must remain intact so that every customer, no matter where they came from, can get what they want when they enter the franchise.

Product Quality

This is the backbone of franchising. The ability for a customer to get the same products or services in hundreds, or even thousands, of locations is what brings the customers through the doors. But in order to insure a positive and enjoyable experience, they must receive those products and services with the same quality no matter where they purchase them.

If one franchise owner changes the ingredients or the quality of workmanship or the features of any of their products, customers might be disappointed that they did not receive what they purchased last time.

If the quality is lower they may never come back in the future. If the quality is much higher, they will wonder why they didn't get that quality before and they will develop a negative feeling because of that as well.

Franchises have specific rules and procedures to insure that all products and services have the same level of quality and are produced the same way from location to location. This not only protects the customer against widely varying quality but also helps protect the brand name value and image at the same time.

Similar Level of Service

Service is a highly subjective term and a big part of how service is measured is by perception. But things like staffing levels, having the right looking and behaving people to help the customer are all things that are in the control of the franchise owners.

The owner should make every effort to provide the best level of service that the business can provide. Naturally the level of service will be influenced by the type of quality of products that you provide but every business, no matter what they sell, should treat every customer with dignity and respect and in an overall positive manner.

Similar Pricing

Another benefit of owning a franchise is the pricing structure of the products you sell. The customer who has visited a franchise before has an idea of what price levels they are likely to encounter when they walk through the door. This can be a huge positive influence when it comes to larger families or people on a tight budget.

If you own a food service franchise, people will pretty much know how much an item is going to cost before they walk through the doors. If they have kids, they will know that each child can eat for less than $5 where the no name place down the street could be $5 or might be $15! This can be a powerful draw for your business.

Franchises usually suggest pricing levels and some franchises may tightly control those prices. There might be slight differences between metropolitan areas and rural areas because of higher costs but for the most part, you will know what to expect before you actually walk in.

Everything we discussed in this chapter is designed to accomplish one thing. That is to instill confidence and peace of mind in the customer. They want to be assured that they will get the same products in Florida that they will get in Oregon and vice versa.

When you consider that some of the largest businesses in the world today are franchises built on this exact same premise, it is hard to dispute the value of providing a uniform level of experience at your location as well.

Market, Market, Market

The key for any business, franchise or otherwise, is visibility. For a new business, visibility is more than just a key, it is absolutely critical. New businesses have the problem of getting people aware that they now exist. Even if people know they exist, they might not be aware of the type of business it is or what products or services they sell.

For new businesses, we have to overcome the fact that people usually continue to shop where they currently shop unless they are given a reason or incentive to go somewhere else. So even though you might have the lowest prices, the best selection and are the most customer friendly business in town, many people will never know that because they never will set foot through your doors.

New businesses also have the issue of money when it comes to advertising and marketing. Most established businesses earmark a percentage of their profits for advertising. When this happens previous sales pay for future advertising so there is no sacrifice or out of the owners pocket cost for that advertising. After a while it is like the expense isn't even there. It has become a habit and no one even thinks about it anymore. For a brand new business though, money can be an issue.

Advertising is not cheap. In fact, cheap advertising is usually not a good idea anyway because if your advertising doesn't reach anyone, it doesn't do you any good. Since advertising is priced according to quality and audience exposure, good advertising might be expensive. With advertising, the saying "You get what you pay for." Is really true!

A brand new business does not have sales to pay for advertising. A new business MUST advertise now to get sales later and to raise awareness of your business in the community. Even if the advertising does not produce sales now, if it makes people aware that you exist, and if it helps bring people through the door if only to look around, it has done its purpose.

Every new business must have money set aside for the early advertising it needs to do to help establish itself.

In fact, advertising should be one of the things we research before going into business so we get an idea of how much money we need to have on hand. After all, if you have enough money to get your business open but then have nothing left to let people know you are open that can present a real problem.

One of the huge mistakes a lot of people make when they open their business is to skimp on advertising because of the costs involved. They feel that they will wait until they generate sales that can help pay for advertising. It is their way of saving money now while sales are lower and not covering expenses.

While it is good to be frugal and watch expenses in the beginning months of your business, one of the areas where you NEED to spend money is on advertising. In fact many businesses spend MORE on advertising when they first open than they will later! Saturation buying of advertising in the beginning will help bring more people through the doors in less time than a small campaign would.

Here are just a few of the main reasons a new business should not skimp on their marketing:

Awareness

In the very beginning, advertising is how new businesses let the public know they are open for business and ready to serve them. Depending on where a business is located, many people might not go past the business as it was being built or getting ready to open. So advertising is the only way to make these people aware that you exist and are ready to help them.

In areas where large geographical spaces are served by one town or business area, advertising might be the only way some folks hear about your business. That is because they might only visit the town every few weeks or months. And even then they might not go by where your business is being built.

Education

Advertising allows the business owner to educate the public on what type of business they have and what kinds of products and services they offer to their customers. Though most of the time when it comes to franchises this is already known, advertising helps make it clear what customers can expect to find in your store.

Product Awareness

Advertising allows you to highlight particular products and services, explain their purpose and why the customer might need them.

While some products and services are well known there are many others that people are not aware of and many problems that have solutions the customers are not aware of either.

Unique Selling Position

Every successful business has reasons why it is better than the competition. But those reasons aren't much good when no one knows about them. Advertising allows the business owner to tell people why they are better than anyone else.

Advertising can stress things like free delivery, longer hours, lower prices, value added services like free installation and other things can often mean the different between customers going to your store or going somewhere else. Advertising allows you to bring these things to the front of the customer's eyes and help make sure they are aware of all that you have to offer.

Anticipation

One of the things many business owners do is build excitement and anticipation for their business by advertising before they are ready to open their doors. Purchasing advertising and signage letting people know something new is coming soon makes people aware of your business and anxiously await the opening.

This will create a "buzz" in the community as people wait for you to open. This is especially useful when franchises are involved because people might be excited to finally get that franchise in their neighborhood. If you use advertising correctly before you open, you can have a flood of people waiting for your doors to open on opening day!

Pricing

When it comes to pricing, advertising allows you to accomplish two goals. First, it makes people aware of the overall pricing structure of your business. It lets them know if you are a higher priced business or a lower cost business. This helps people pick and choose the right places to shop and also makes it easier on you when people know what to expect before they come in.

Second, advertising allows the business to inform people about specials and sales they are running where prices are reduced. This is what most people think about when they are asked about advertising. They think about sales, promotions and saving money.

Announcements

Advertising can also be used to announce important things about your business.

This might be a grand opening, an upcoming event, your next sale, or to announce the arrival of an eagerly anticipated product that is now available for your customers.

Examples of this type of advertisement might be for the upcoming 4th of July Sale, a Grand Opening, or the arrival of the latest generation phone. Hair Salons regularly use advertisement sot announce a new stylist who has just joined their staff.

At its most basic level advertising is used to convey information regarding to you and your business to the people in the area that you hope will become your customers.

There are many forms of advertising and each for has its own pluses and minuses and each one will be better for certain industries or type of businesses. There are many marketing and advertising companies around who will be happy to discuss the options available to you and your business in your area.

Your franchise company will also have a track record of which types of advertising works best and may have marketing professionals on staff to help you with your marketing. If they have people to help you then use them.

Depending on your particular franchise, you may also have the opportunity to participate in group advertising which is great because when several owners in an area pool their marketing resources they can purchase more advertising at less cost. Sometimes part of your franchise fees include this kind of advertising as well.

Whatever you do just make sure not to fall into the trap many new business owners fall into. Do not skimp on advertising to save money. This will usually back fire on you and make it more difficult and take longer for your business to turn profitable. Look for ways to cut other expenses but make sure you market properly and effectively and continue doing that for as long as you remain in business.

Conclusion

Hopefully by now you have a pretty good idea when it comes to making a few important decisions. The purpose of this book was not to make the decisions for you because everyone and every situation are different. However, by giving you the information and knowledge to help you make the best decisions, this book will hopefully save you time, money and aggravation.

For some franchising is the answer to some of their biggest obstacles when it comes to starting their own business. To be given something that is proven to work, and the help to get it started and profitable, is not something to be taken lightly. But there are costs associated with all of this help and those must be considered carefully in the decision making process.

For others, franchising might be too restrictive and might even stifle the creativity of the owner. The rules and regulations and restrictions placed on the owners might be too hard to follow. They might even be totally opposite to how you feel about running your business. It is up to you to decide who you are and how well the franchise fits not only into your financial position but to your philosophy as well. Both are extremely important.

Also understand that all franchises are not created equal and you need to understand exactly what you are getting into before you join. Finding out something afterwards might be too late! Generally speaking, the more established and well known and respected franchises will carry a larger price tag. In other words, you get what you pay for. But that larger price tag might give you much higher sales and eventually make you more money that a less expensive franchise.

When it comes to profits and money, we cannot stress enough the need for having a GOOD accountant on your side. Not your uncle Sid who took a bookkeeping course in adult education. You want an established accountant, hopefully a CPA, who has the skills and knowledge to advise you properly.

The same goes for having a good lawyer on your team before you sign any documents or contracts.

Protecting your rights in the very beginning can save you a boat load of money and aggravation later. Look for an attorney experienced in franchise and business law so that they will have the expertise you need when you need it.

But the very best advice we have to offer you is two-fold.

First, make decisions based on what is right for you, not someone else. Everybody is different and what worked for your cousin Elroy might be a disaster for you. Know yourself and what you like and enjoy. Know what you are good at, and equally important, know what you are not so good at. No one is great at everything but those who know exactly who and what they are will be the ones with the greatest chance of success.

Second, surround yourself with people who have skills and knowledge that is better or more thorough than yours. Let them help you become successful. Let them teach you and be a sponge when it comes to learning everything you possibly can from them. Very few people made it to the top by themselves. They might have had a great idea or a wonderful product but it probably took a ton of people to bring everything together and make it a success!

Franchising is not a license to print money and no business is guaranteed to succeed.

But for those who want a team behind them as they start and open their business, franchising might be the perfect solution. Just go into it with your eyes wide open and be honest with yourself every step of the way.

www.ingramcontent.com/pod-product-compliance
Lightning Source LLC
Chambersburg PA
CBHW051445170526
45166CB00001B/122